James Payn

The Retrosprect - A Glance

Thirty years of the history

James Payn

The Retrosprect - A Glance
Thirty years of the history

ISBN/EAN: 9783744780179

Printed in Europe, USA, Canada, Australia, Japan

Cover: Foto ©Lupo / pixelio.de

More available books at **www.hansebooks.com**

HOWARD STREET M. E. CHURCH.

—AT—

THIRTY YEARS OF THE HISTORY

—OF—

HOWARD STREET

Methodist Episcopal Church,

OF SAN FRANCISCO.

PUBLISHED BY THE OFFICIAL BOARD

A. BUSWELL & CO. PRINTERS AND BINDERS.
SAN FRANCISCO,
1883.

PRESIDENT BOARD OF TRUSTEES

ORIGINAL MEMBERS.

The following names appear as original or organizing members of the Church:

M. E. Willing.	Horace Hoag.
Seneca Jones.	James Christy.
Elizabeth Jones.	Charles Merriman.
Wm. H. Codington.	John Payne.
Clayton Tweed.	Wm. Hatzel.
John Johnson.	Jas. W. Whiting.
Eliza J. Johnson.	Anne Whiting.
Elizabeth Winters.	Ellen Freeborn.
John Winters.	Judah Alden.
John Sims.	Samuel Perkins.
Elizabeth Christy.	T. G. Merrill.

T. H. Hickey.

OFFICERS.

The following is a chronological list of official members from the organization to the present time:

TRUSTEES.

R. P. Spire.
Henry Read.
D. L. Ross.
J. B. Bond.
Wm. Phillips.
Horace Hoag.
J. E. Whitcher.
Seneca Jones.
Franklin Kinsman.
John C. Ayres.
John Paine.
Edward L. Smith.
Charles Merriman.
Wm. H. Codington.
Edward R. Samis.
L. S. Ely.
Robert Stitt.
Fred. A. Beardsley.
Edward McLean.
Chas. Goodall.
Henry Thomas.
J. W. Whiting.
D. S. Howard.
Samuel Hancock.
James Harlow.
Wm. H. Gawley.
Robt. McElroy.
R. G. Byxbee.
W. H. Howland.
John Curry.
S. S. Sprague.
H. H. Noble.
Sam'l Mosgrove.
J. F. Byxbee.
John M. Buffington.
Andrew Nelson.
D. O. Shattuck.

STEWARDS.

M. E. Willing.
Seneca Jones.
James Christie.
Horace Hoag.
W. H. Codington.
John Paine.
Chas. Merriman.
Simeon Jenkins.
John C. Ayres.
E. L. Smith.
F. A. Beardsley.
D. B. Finch.
Edward McLean.
M. C. Dodge.
Felix Sanchez.
Henry Thomas.
Chas. Goodall.
S S Sprague
H G. Blasdell.
D. S. Howard.
J. F. Byxbee.
Ames Arnold.
John A. Carter.
J. M. Buffington.
Wm. Bartling.
Joseph Knowland.
H. H. Noble.
W. F. Kellett.

C. C. Lombard.
Sam'l Mosgrove.
J. J. Applegate.
Chas. Lenoir.
Andrew Nelson.
Daniel Grant.
Thomas Penlington.
J. R. Merrill.
Wm. Perkins.
J. B. Firth.
J. W. Duncan.
G. S. Keys.
Wm. Harover.
Geo. B Adair.
F. A. Nickerson.
Chas A. Sankey.
Geo. Penlington.
W. H. Porter.
T. O. Lewis.
J. W. H. Campbell.
Andrew Wilson.
Robert Gemmell.
Chas. Jones.
J. K. Jones.
Chas. B. Perkins.
Frederick Peterson.
J. C. Smith.
J. G. Whittington.

E. L. Barber.

OFFICERS.

CLASS LEADERS.

Chas. Merriman.
Thos. Welch
Robert Stitt.
Robt. McElroy.
Henry Thomas.
A. F. Hitchcock.
John Arnold.
James F. Smith.
D. S. Howard.
Sam'l McHenry.
W. H. Codington.
H. Perkins.
J. W. Whiting.
Francis Mitchell.
E. L. Smith.
J. W. Bluett.

Daniel Grant.
Edwin Cutting.
J. J. Applegate.
Mrs. E. Cutting.
Mrs E Firth.
Seneca Jones.
J. M. Buffington
C. J. Moyes.
J. A. Bergner.
P. C. Miller.
Ezra Smith.
Mrs. T. O. Lewis.
E. V. Hull.
Alex. Head.
Henry Large.
K. W. Gress.

Chas. Jones.

PRESENT MEMBERS.

The following is the list of members at the present time:

Appelgate, J. J.
Appelgate, Annie S.
Acheson, Betsey
Anglein, Rebecca
Adair, Geo. B.
Adair, Mattie E.
Armstrong, Matilda
Allen, Charlotte
Anderson, Aurora
Allison, H. H.
Akeson, Annie
Allen, Maggie
Allen, Mary W.
Atthouse, Sarah J.
Ambrose, William
Ayers, Lottie
Bixby, John F.
Bixby, Maggie
Bixby, Edward M.
Biggs, Mehetable
Bartlett, Eliza
Bartlett, Eliza
Bartlett, Bertie
Balcom, Lydia A.
Bordwell, Helen
Bergland, Hans
Bergland, Annie C.
Blanchard, Candace
Bretteville, Harrison
Burleigh, Robertson

Burleigh, Margaret J.
Burleigh, Edward
Bergner, Annie
Black, Sara A.
Black, Hettie
Brown, Mrs. Bessie
Brown, Emma
Brown, Bessie
Brown, Harriet
Boyle, Nettie M.
Bell, Mary
Batchelder, T. N.
Batchelder, Mrs. T. N.
Batchelder, Clara Bell
Bowman, Mary E.
Bowman, Emma
Beach, Emma
Barker, Grace
Brundage, Mrs.
Bower, Adah
Bunyan, Edward T.
Buckman, Frank W.
Buckman, Nettie C.
Benzon, Fisher Von
Boucher, Fannie
Berry, Mary F.
Bell, Lucy Jane
Cady, Sophia
Campbell, J. W. H.
Campbell, Emily

PRESENT MEMBERS.

Curry, John
Curry, Margaret
Cady, Mary C.
Caine, Thos. W.
Caine, John
Cordey, John
Cordey, Mrs. J.
Cummings, W. F.
Cannon, Mrs. J. S.
Cook, F. C.
Cook, Mrs. M. N.
Cox, H. (D. D.)
Cox, Philip K.
Cox, Sarah
Cornell, Eliza
Cornell, Miss E. M.
Conley, Agnes
Cowan, Stephen
Chatfield, Sarah
Crall, H. J.
Crane, Frederick
Cease, Lodema
Callow, Chas. W.
Caley, Robert
Cooke, James B.
Cloud, Andrew J.
Cloud, Mrs. A. C.
Cluff, Idarene
Darling, Richard
Dawson, George
Davis, Thos. B.
Donaldson, W. G.
Davy, Mariah S.
Dawson, J. W.
Draper, Emerson H.
Davis, Wm.
Draper, John H.
Dewitt, Sarah A.
Derosier, Charles
Dowd, Mrs. A. A.
Dawe, Annie N.
Dunnigan, W. G.

Damrell, Sarah
Donellon, B. C.
Donellon, A.
Davey, Mrs. Emma
Emory, Rebecca
Elford, Henrietta
Firth, J. B.
Firth, Eliza
Filebrown, Mrs. A. B.
Foster, Emily
Filben, Thos. (Rev.)
Ferguson, Thos.
Ferguson, Alice
Foss, H. M. B.
Fredericks, Emma
Friend, Elizabeth
Fay, Nellie
Goodall, Charles
Goodall, Serena
Gardner, Mrs. L. G.
Goodall, Rosa
Gordon, Annie
Good, Mrs. L. B.
Girvin, Hannah
Gress, K. Wellington
Graves, Sarah H.
Gliddon, Georgie
Grover, Thomas
Grey, James M.
Guthrie, H. William
Gardiner, Thos.
Hancock, Samuel
Hancock, Mrs. E.
Hancock, Robert
Howland, Mrs. E.
Howland, Lucinda
Hessel, Mrs. G.
Hess, A. J.
Hanson, Elizabeth A.
Hare, Amelia
Hare, Emma
Hall, Sarah N.

PRESENT MEMBERS. 11

Heath, Eugenia
Hasty, Minnie
Harris, Wm. J.
Harris, Emma Birdella
Harris, Clyde
Harris, Matthew
Harris, Jeannette
Hawver, William
Head, Elizabeth
Head, Louise E.
Head, Fred.
Head, Jeannie
Hoffaker, Sarah E.
Haylard, Peter
Hichens, Ellen
Haughton, Mary
Inman, William
Jantzen, Frederick
Jantzen, Caroline
Jantzen, Fred. J.
Jantzen, Wm.
Jantzen, Carrie
Jantzen, Dora F. C.
Jones, Seneca
Jones, Elizabeth
Jones, Joseph K.
Jones, Kate
Jones, Sallie
Jones, Charles
Jones, Emma
Jones, Chas. J.
Jones, Mary S.
Jones, Laura
Jones, John
Jones, Mary
Jones, Margaret
Jones, Kate
Jones, Eliza
Jones, Delilah
Jones, Annie
Jones, Tillie
Johnson, Elizabeth

Johnson, John
Johnson, Miss E.
Jocelyn, Mrs.
Jewell, Lottie B.
Jewell, Addie J.
Kinsman, Franklin
Kinsman, Eliza
Keys, Mary M.
Kennet, Wm.
Kennet, Sarah J.
Keys, Alice
King, Margaret
King, Margaret S.
Koster, John E.
Kanouse, Carrie
Koopman, Catherine
Kline, Elizabeth
Kline, Julia
Kentfield, Mrs. J.
Lindsay, Fulton
Lamb, Marietta
Lattimer, George
Lattimer, Sarah
Lattimer, Willie
Lattimer, George
Luders, Joseph
Lesley, William
Landis, Amanda
Lautermilch, Mrs. M. H.
Latham, Joseph
Latham, Mary
Lawrence, Mrs.
Large, Henry
Large, Mary J.
Linn, Mrs. M.
Lane, Mrs. Mary
Lane, Lizzie
Lubeck, Hattie
Lyons, Catherine A.
Lowel Emma J.
Lowrey, Amanda
Lowrey, Delilah A.

PRESENT MEMBERS.

McElroy, Robt. (Rev.)
McElroy, Amanda R.
Merrill, John R.
Merrill, Lucy B.
Miller, Peter C.
Miller, Mrs. P. C.
Miller, Jennie
Mackin, Mrs. A. M.
Minturn, Elizabeth
McFaden, David
McFaden, Eliza
McFaden, Ellie
Mitchell, Francis
Mitchell, James H.
Mitchell, Laura
Mitchell, May
Markley, Rosaline
Macomber, James
Moyes, Chas. J.
Mills, Mrs. H. B.
Mealey, George
McGladery, Miss
Moore, James R.
Morritt, Mrs. W.
Mincher, Isaac
Mincher, Mrs. I.
Mayhew, Ida
McGuire, Alice
Maulfair, Mary A.
Miller, H. W.
Marvin, Stephen B.
Morrow, Lizzie
McDonald, Neil T.
McDonald, Elizabeth
Melvin, Sophie
Maclay, Sarah A.
Noble, H. H.
Nelson, Andrew
Nelson, Elizabeth
Nelson, Emily
Nelson, Sarah
Nickerson, F. A.

Nickerson, Eliza
Nickerson, Agnes
Notley, Maria
Norris, Richard
Over, Andrew
Osgood, Charles
Ovens, William
Ovens, Margaret Jessie
O'Meara, Annie
Oyler, John W.
Peterson, Frederick
Peterson, Hannah F.
Perkins, William
Perkins, Lydia
Perkins, Chas. E.
Perkins, Clara F.
Perkins, William F.
Perkins, Annie
Porter, Wm. H.
Porter, Margaret C.
Percy, Jane
Peacock, Amos
Peacock, Alzurah
Page, Delphine
Palmer, W. F.
Perry, Lois Acelia
Perry, Herman F
Pengelly, Richard
Pengelly, Lizzie
Priest, Alice M.
Philp, John
Philp, Annie S.
Pawning, Carrie
Patterson, Mary
Reynolds, Alice
Reynolds, Mary W.
Rice, Mrs. A. W.
Reagan, John
Reagan, Aurelia
Reagan, Theresa
Roberts, Aggie A.
Rogers, Bella A.

PRESENT MEMBERS. 13

Richardson, Judith
Robertson, Archibald
Robertson, Mrs. A.
Robertson, Thos. J.
Robertson, Edith
Rowe, Katie
Rowe, Hattie
Rowe, Jennie B.
Reagan, Lillie
Riley, John F.
Stitt, Robert
Stitt, Joanna C.
Stitt, John H.
Stitt, Robert J.
Stitt, Annie
Smith, E. L.
Smith, Huldah G.
Sankey, Jeremiah
Sankey, Katie
Stringer, Ida
Salisbury, Mary F.
Scherer, Eliza M.
Scherer, Mary
Stuart, Susan B.
Stuart, Frankie B.
Smith, Geo. W.
Smith, T. B.
Smith, Marian
Smith, Jeremiah
Smith, J. C.
Smith, Mrs. J. C.
Scott, Margaret
Scott, Belle
Simpson, Mrs. Abbie L.
Stuart, John
Shaw, Dillie
Snyder, Mrs. E. L.
Stayton, Sarah
Stodart, Mrs. S. A.
Silva, Julia
Stein, J. E. D.
Stein, Flora

Smith, Elvira R.
Shields, Oscar W.
Smith, Stephen
Sephton, Henry
Sephton, Victoria
Shillcock, Hester
Showers, Andrew
Sinkinson, Elizabeth
Shepard, Matilda
Santee, Levi
Santee, Ina
Stoner, F. J.
Smith, Mary H.
Schultze, Julia
Sprague, Abbie F.
Smith, Mary
Townsend, Sarah
Thomas, Henry
Thomas, Mary A.
Tucker, Henrietta S.
Thompson, Martha
Turnbull, Maria C.
Terschuran, Mrs. M. J.
Taggart, Mrs. Clayton
Thompson, Annie R.
Telyea, Joseph
Telyea, Martha
Thornton, Richard
Tarpley, Lindsey B.
Tarpley, Mrs. S. C.
Tillson, Wm. H.
Taylor, Mabel
Tinnin, Belle
Teague, William
Vaughn, Harmon B.
Vaughn, Sophia
Whiting, James W.
Whiting, Annie
Whittington, John
Whittington, Margaret
Whittington, John C.
Warburton, Mrs. M.

PRESENT MEMBERS.

Walker, Mrs. Jane
Williams, Mrs. H. E.
Williams, John A.
Williams, Sallie F.
Williams, John W.
Williams, Jane E.
Williams, Geo. A.
Williams, Mrs. G. A.
Williams, Mrs. J. F.
Williams, Nellie
Wilson, Andrew
Wilson, J. W. R.
Walker, W. H.

Winn, C. C.
Winn, Mrs. H. S.
Whittaker, Wm.
Whittaker, Nellie
Whittaker, Lottie
Wagner, Harr
Walkington, Eliza
Walkington, Estelle M.
Waddell, Robert
Watson, Jane
White, Lizzie
Worth, Nellie M.
Worth, Capt.

J. M. BUFFINGTON.

INTRODUCTION.

When we resolved to observe a day of thanksgiving for emancipation from the thralldom of a debt which had mercilessly goaded us on in interest-paying until its inflictions had become well nigh unbearable, we had no purpose of issuing a memorial volume, such as we now present to our friends and the members of the church. It was while we were in the midst of our rejoicings, that a former pastor, who had a part assigned him in the programme, suggested that the "Milestone" paper furnished by Robert. McElroy should be embalmed in the "art immortal," and given to all the church members. The idea found favor with all who heard it, and it was then and there resolved to print the paper referred to in pamphlet form. Subsequently a committee was chosen by the official board to carry forward the proposition, and the material which asked and merited a place in the pamphlet began to accumulate until it was far too formidable for the form proposed, and the book form was agreed upon. Subsequent action by the Quarterly Conference provided for its publication, and gave the committee full power in the matter. A Conference Historical Society, which has for years been pleading with the churches to furnish sketches of history and incident, will recognize this as in keeping with its designs and desires; and we assay this humble effort with the hope that others of our churches which organized early will follow in some way that will furnish the archives of the Society with the material it seeks.

The services which called out the principal article contained in this little volume were held in the church August 12th, 1883, and consisted of a Love-Feast service at 9.30 A. M., led by the Rev. S. D. Simonds, one of the earliest pastors; a Milestone service at 11 A. M., at which time Robert McElroy furnished the address referred to above, and which appears first in the series of articles ; and an evening service of short addresses by the former pastors present.

Of the church decorations for the occasion, a reporter of one of the city papers says the interior of the edifice presented a

INTRODUCTION. 17

beautiful but chaste appearance. The base of the reading-desk was enveloped with a profusion of ferns, smilax, and flowers. On the top of the reading-desk, in front of the Bible, was a unique, gold-gilted vase of fuchsias. On each side of the pulpit was a slender tripod, adorned with variegated flowers; in niches each side, in rear of the pulpit, were exhibited deciduous greenhouse shrubs. Immediately over the center of the rostrum, suspended in front of the organ gallery, was a beautiful life-size, gold-mounted portrait of the Rev. J. D. Blain, who was instrumental in the erection of this church. The librarians of the Sunday-school are credited with the artistic taste revealed in the decorations. And adds, only four members are to-day connected with the church that were members when the church was erected in 1851. Seated on the platform were the Rev. Dr. H. Cox, Rev. S. D. Simonds, Rev. J. A. Bruner of Chico, Rev. W. S. Urmy of Modesto, Rev. D. A. Dryden, Rev. Dr. F. F. Jewell, the present pastor; being the only pastors alive (but one) of the fourteen which have held the pastorate of this church since its organization.

After the general opening, Dr. Jewell

spoke feelingly of a number of congratulatory notes which he had been the recipient of from sister churches, and more especially of one received from Brother Dille, pastor of the Central M. E. Church. He deeply regretted the absence of Dr. Briggs, late pastor of this church, who was to have delivered a brief address, but unfortunately his ministerial duties detained him. Rev. D. A. Dryden compared the life of a church to that of a child—its birth, progressiveness, and final maturity. Some at birth are very feeble and poor, others of more auspicious circumstances are born, as it were, with a gold spoon in their mouths. Mr. Dryden expressed a conviction and belief as to the real source and final prosperity of the Howard Street M. E. Church, and credited the ultimate success of the church to the late Rev. J. D. Blain.

Rev. W. S. Urmy said: "It is a pleasant thing to be here with you and unite in the Jubilee services. Next Thursday will be the 16th of August; thirty years ago that day I arrived in San Francisco from New York. I recall with ecstasy the happy days spent in our place of worship in Happy Valley, which stood near Mission Street, and not near Market Street, as Brother McElroy said this morning; it was in the hollow nearer Rincon Hill." He paid a compliment to the pillars of the church for their support during his pastorate.

Captain Charles Goodall smilingly ascended the rostrum, and in a genial manner said: "I am not an old member, although not a young man—that is to say, not so old in membership as some assembled here tonight. It is a quarter of a century since I became an official member of this church. Brother Urmy, as he informs you, was a young man then, with raven locks, which have since whitened with advancing years. We were just then coming to be prosperous; even then I know of a kind sister who frequently came down to the Folsom Street church with a broom, and even brought candles. Our church was once so poor that Dr. Bannister came into church on some occasions and preached without breakfast. These were hard times with us. The first time I had the honor of forming an extensive opinion of the benevolent qualities of the late Rev. Brother Blain was in my office. One morning a bummer, or tramp, entered and endeavored to negotiate the loan of fifty cents, and the tramp was not long in seeing the street; but what was my surprise, a few minutes later, when he entered with Brother Blain, who asked for pen and ink, and wrote an order for the aforesaid tramp to get a meal at the Hillman House.

"I remonstrated with Brother Blain, and informed him of the true character of the individual. However, he said, 'I cannot see a poor fellow being in want of bread.' This tramp proceeded to the hotel and demolished a square meal, and then went to Mr. Smith, the clerk, and demanded a quarter change on the order, stating he had an order for a four bit meal, and did not get a quarter's worth; the result was, the tramp picked himself up in the street.

Rev. J. A. Bruner in a pleasing manner informed the audience of the reception extended to him on his arrival from Marysville. He was met by a delegation of members, which consisted of Brothers Goodall, McElroy, and Codington, who waited three days for him and his family. "The church was prosperous in those days," he said; "I learned to love it, and God was with us, as he will be at the Grand Jubilee, when the books shall be opened to judge the world."

Rev. S. D. Simonds excused himself from speaking on account of the lateness of the hour: "but," said he, "I will present a specimen brick. You may have an eloquent preacher or speaker—in fact, I like to hear one myself; you may have a profound theologian; you may have friendly socials— but if you have not the grace of God in your hearts, it availeth nothing."

Rev. Dr. H. Cox succeeded Brother Peck at this church, after persistent appeals from Bishop Baker and Bishop Kingsley. Dr. Cox spoke of the revival which followed his wake to the church, and graphically portrayed the number of hundreds that found grace at this selfsame altar. The reverend gentleman continuing, said: "I never preached here without a breakfast [and placing his hand across his body], nor without a dinner either, which I suppose you all can guess [laughter]; I always had the greatest delicacies that California could produce."

Dr. Jewell concluded the Jubilee by briefly describing the pleasure he has derived by five years' pastorate.

Some of the data furnished will be necessarily duplicated, as the history of the church and Sunday-school are separately furnished and prepared by different hands. Other portraits of those whose services would plead for an appearance in the volume have been sought but could not be obtained. That the unity and symmetry which should characterize and would appear in a volume written by a single pen are lacking here, we concede and yet do not regret, as the purpose is to furnish incident and give permanent record to events connected with the early struggles and conquests of Methodism in San Francisco. It is not intended for general circulation, but rather to remain in the families of our communion, as a hand-book and manual to furnish inspiration and awaken gratitude in the hearts of our church family.

To the members and friends of the Howard Street Methodist Episcopal Church this volume is affectionately inscribed by

THE COMMITTEE.

R. McELROY.
Treasurer Board Trustees.

HISTORICAL SKETCH.

BY R. MCELROY.

This society came into being in 1851. Its early history was fraught with severe struggle and great uncertainty. At that time San Francisco society was in a very crude condition. It was made up of people from every nation under the sun, most of whom had no fear of God or disposition to serve him. Indeed, the mass were wholly given up to the practice of profligacy and irreligion. The absorbing passion was for gold, and perhaps there is no passion of the human breast so absorbing and so intensely demoralizing as this insatiate greed for gold. It stops not at any cost to secure its object. It does not hesitate to sacrifice everything that is noble and godlike in man's nature to gratify its quenchless longings. It reduces its victim to a cringing sycophant or demonizes him into a remorseless fiend. It robs him of all individual comfort, and makes him the veriest galley-slave to toil. It wears out every

fiber of the body, every faculty of the
mind, and every heaven-born aspiration of
the soul. It engenders plottings the most
vicious, schemes the most unscrupulous,
and deeds the most dark and damning. It
is a stranger alike to mercy and justice.
It heeds not the cry of the needy, nor has
it any pity for the oppressed. It is sordid
to the last degree, selfish without the
thought of another, and stony as the very
adamant. Under its stimulus, virtue be-
comes a matter of merchandise, and every
lofty impulse of the human heart paralyzed
and dead. Where it reigns supreme all
honor is gone, all honesty at an end, all
virtue no more, and all veracity buried in
Lethe's deepest waters. Surely, no truth
of Holy Writ stands out in bolder relief or
is more fully drawn to the life than that
" the love of money is the root of all evil."

For gold most of the then population had
left their homes in other lands; for this they
had sundered every sacred tie, had bid
farewell to wives and children, had abandoned churches and church relationships,
had sacrificed farms and homesteads; and
so, when they reached this city, gold *must*
be secured—no matter how or at what cost
of brain or muscle, of personal dignity or

self-respect; no matter what violation of conscience or wreck of moral principle was deemed necessary to capture this beau-ideal of all ambition — the sacrifice, however great and terrible, was most freely made. Gold must be had by fair means or by foul. This was the ingrain sentiment of the community. No wonder, then, that many who in other lands had borne the sacred name of Christian, and even minister of Christ, now abandoned themselves to all manner of flagrant sin, and became the vilest of the vile; no wonder that every street, both night and day, resounded with swelling strains of band music to lure the simple into haunts of vice; no wonder that open doors of gambling-houses were seen on every hand; no wonder that faro-banks and games of chance were as much a matter of open business as were the sale of merchandise or the pursuit of any legitimate calling. Nor was it a matter of wonder that murder and robbery were of almost daily occurrence, and were looked upon as comparatively innocent amusements. Of course these crimes were but a certain process of making money, and was not making money perfectly legitimate? If a man would not stand up and deliver his money to the footpad, why, of course he ought to be murdered for his want of magnanimity. And so natural law was constantly invaded, and the natural rights of man incessantly violated, all under the driving force of this absorbing passion for gold. How unfriendly, then, was such a public sentiment to any organization which had for its object the suppression of vice and the reformation of the vicious! How utterly indisposed were a people ruled and entirely under the dominion of so base a passion to aid any party in the promotion of pure and undefiled religion!

Another reason which made church work in those days so exceedingly difficult was the universal purpose on the part of the people to leave the country just as soon as they could wring success out of their opportunities. No one came to build up a permanent business or a permanent home. Not a man could be found who did not intend immediately after making his "pile" to return to his home, be that home in whatever part of the world it might. This State was a mere place of sojourn, where no one considered himself a citizen, and where no anchor held his moorings. Just as soon as the vessel was freighted, the cable was loosed, the sails set and spread to the breeze, and the prow turned toward the port whence she came. So was the population ever shifting; so were the elements from which organizations were to be built, if built at all, ever eluding your grasp, for even the unsuccessful were constantly migrating. From one mining section to another, from city to city, from town to town, and from camp to camp, so did the human tide constantly surge. With pick and shovel, with pan and blanket, the moving mass trod its weary way through scorching heat and drenching rain, in eager pursuit of the shining dust. No other thought absorbed the brain but how that dust could be amassed and carried back to that home in the far East, where the wife sat in lonely expectancy, and the children left their play and asked in vain for him who had been the joy of their young life and the hope of their advancing years. Talk to such an one about organizing a church or establishing religious services in the place of his sojourn, even though he had a church letter in his pocket, and he would turn a deaf ear to your entreaty, or solemnly assure you that here he had no abiding-place, and hence had no need for a church home in these ends of the earth.

But notwithstanding all these discouragements, a few devout ones, under the lead of Rev. W. Taylor, the pioneer Methodist preacher of this coast, determined to organize themselves into a society which should be known as the Second M. E. Church of San Francisco. The organization, however, was not complete until January, 1852, when the Rev. M. C. Briggs became its pastor, and the Happy Valley schoolhouse, which stood about where the Grand Hotel now stands, its temporary habitation. The number of its original members was twenty-three, four of whom remain with us till this day. These are Brother and Sister J. W. Whiting, and Brother and Sister Seneca Jones. The others are mostly with the Master in the skies, where they rest from their labors, but have left the rich fruit of their devotion for us to enjoy.

Foremost among this little band was Rev. M. E. Willing, a local elder, who came to this coast at that early day to represent the book interest of the church. This man of God was at once recognized as the lay leader of the little society; and by his wise counsels and energetic measures, conduced very much to its early prosperity. He was its first class-leader, its first recording steward, and its second Sunday-school superintendent. His return to the Atlantic States in the latter part of 1852 was a great loss to the society; but his memory is still cherished among us as a man who stood bravely against the torrent of worldliness and lifted high the banner of the Cross in the midst of California's intensest Mammon-worship.

This little flock went to work with true California energy to build up a church whose influence would be felt for good in the midst of the prevailing ungodliness, but their numbers were few and their means limited. Their pastor was gifted with unusual ability, but other duties claimed a part of his service, as he was also one of the editors of the " California Christian Advocate," the publication of which began in October, 1851. He however gave the society all the service possible, preaching with great acceptability every Sabbath until about the first of March, 1852, when he was called East on a two-fold mission: first, to attend the General Conference which convened in Boston in May of that year; and second, to join his destiny to one who has since been to him, through all these thirty years of married life, a constant baptism of blessedness, and to the church an ever-increasing benediction. The little society, however, was not left without a pastor, for about that time the Rev. George S. Phillips came at the bidding of the authorities of the church to this coast, and was immediately placed in charge, to remain during the pastor's absence. Brother Phillips gave himself fully to the work of the church, and was exceedingly efficient in both pulpit and pastorate. Meantime, the membership was increased by parties who were constantly arriving from the East with church letters, insomuch that the little schoolhouse became too inconvenient for the congregation, and the question of church site and church building was forced upon their consideration. A lot on Folsom Street had previously been secured for the society through the efforts of Rev. W. Taylor, but it was then too far from the center of population to be of any service, and so the Board determined to secure a site, if possible, on Market Street, near the place of their meeting. Soon the opportunity arrived, and a large lot was bought and paid for. This was situated on Market Street, and is a part of the ground now covered by the Palace Hotel. We all thought the church had secured a princely estate, but at that time there were no clean titles in the city, as every inch of available space was the battle-ground of many conflicting interests; and to make matters worse, there were but few clean courts who would impartially adjudicate these interests. Many of these were so corrupt that judicial decisions rarely went in favor of justice, but the size of the litigants' "pile" not unfrequently determined the character of the decision. Indeed, many of these decisions had no stability whatever, for they were often reversed almost before the ink had dried upon the paper upon which they had been written. It was very common for even supreme judges to reverse their own decisions, and not unfrequently was this done on the most flimsy pretense and for the most trifling reasons. It was therefore soon discovered that, although the church had honestly bought the lot and paid a full price for it in gold coin, its title must be questioned, and its trustees brought into these courts to defend their right to the property. Not only were they sued at the law, but those who held possession for the church were summarily dispossessed by hired rowdies, who came against them with bludgeons and pistols. Possession being now gone, and that being nine points in law, the case at once became exceedingly dubious. However, it was stoutly contested, both in State and United States courts for a number of years, but at length the old trustees, becoming wearied and worn out with the fruitless and expensive litigation, abandoned the contest, and so this princely property went forever from the grasp of its rightful owner, and thus was practically demonstrated the fearful fact that man *will* rob God.

The pastor, Brother Briggs, returned from his Eastern trip after six months' absence, and resumed his labors in the charge, in connection with his substitute, who also remained his assistant to the end of the year. The General Conference which had recently held its session in Boston had created two Conferences out of the Oregon and California Mission Conference, and henceforth both the Oregon and California Conferences were to be vested with all the rights and privileges of the older Conferences, and Bishop Ames, who had just been elected and ordained by this General Conference, had been appointed to hold the first sessions of these new Conferences.

Accordingly, the Bishop reached this city, in pursuance of his work, in January, 1853. He was joyfully welcomed by every Methodist on the coast, as his arrival was an epoch of momentous interest in the history of our little Zion. He preached his first sermon in California on January 24th, in the Happy Valley schoolhouse, and the service was one of intense interest to all present. The Bishop at this service administered the sacrament of infant baptism. This was the first child baptized in the society. Only think of *infants* in California in the first month of 1853! The family was an exceedingly scarce institution in this community in those days, as most of the population were exclusively men. On this day the Quarterly Conference was held at which the first Board of Trustees was appointed. It consisted of Seneca Jones, Charles Merriman, Horace Hoag, John Payne, W. H. Coddington, J. W. Whiting, and James Christy. Four of these are still living in this city, and two still members of the church. This Quarterly Conference also licensed the first preacher, and recommended him to the Annual Conference. His name was John Bennum. This brother was one of God's

choicest gems, for he was not only very
gifted, but exceedingly sweet-spirited and
thoroughly consecrated to the work of his
Master. He was received by the Annual
Conference and sent to a circuit in the
mines. He had not labored long, however, before he was drowned in attempting
to ford a swollen stream; and so he was
not, for God took him.

The first session of the California Conference convened in the Powell Street Church
February 3rd, 1853. When the appointments were announced, this charge was left
to be supplied, which was a great disappointment to the people, as they had fully
expected the return of their pastor, Brother
Briggs. He however was sent to the
stronger church on Powell Street, and this
little vine had to wait for several weeks for
a vine-dresser to be imported from the
East. The importation, however, arrived,
and it proved to be Rev. N. P. Heath, a
man of fine talent and thorough devotion.
He at once set on foot measures to secure a
house of worship, as there seemed no prospect of permanent success without this.
Up to this time the society had been like
Noah's dove, with no place whereon to
light its weary feet. It had migrated be-

tween the Happy Valley schoolhouse and Music Hall, a public building that stood on Bush Street where now stands the Occidental Hotel. The new pastor determined that this migration should cease by the society utilizing its lot on Folsom Street, by building a church thereon. This, however, was an unwise decision, for the lot was situated amid sand dunes, with scarcely any population about it. If the church, located there, should have any congregation, the people must come from a long distance, and wade through almost impassable sand drifts at that. But notwithstanding these serious objections, the plan was carried out, and $5,000 were borrowed, at three per cent per month interest, with which to build the church. The property was mortgaged for that amount, and from that moment its troubles began. The house was finished and dedicated on January 7th, 1854, and regular services commenced within its walls. There seemed, however, little else than constant discouragement, for the congregation was very small, and the $150 per month interest money which had to be met, together with all other current expenses of the church, weighed so heavily upon the society that it came very near disbanding.

The little band worked nobly, and did all in their power to meet their ever-recurring obligations; but the load was too heavy, and had not the Missionary Society come to their rescue, the whole property would have been sacrificed and the society driven to pieces.

Rev. Dr. Bannister, of precious memory, served as pastor during the Conference year of 1854, and nobly did that royal man endure the privations to which he was subject, that perchance he might save the honor of the cause.

In 1855 Rev. D. A. Dryden was appointed pastor, but as he was unable to live on the wind, he remained in the charge but a little time, and during the balance of the year the pulpit was filled with preachers who gave their services gratuitously.

Meantime, the class meetings were regularly kept up, one of which, under the leadership of Robert Stitt, was held at the residence of Franklin Kinsman, whose house was ever open, like that of Mary and Martha, both to the man of Nazareth and his followers. Father and Mother Kinsman still linger among us, listening patiently for the footfall of the messenger who shall bring the Master's call for them to go up higher, where silvered hairs shall be changed to golden locks, and where the wrinkles of age shall fade into the bloom of eternal youth.

In 1856 Rev. N. P. Heath was again sent to the charge, and the Parent Missionary Society of the M. E. Church made an appropriation of $1,400 to pay the mortgage and save the property from execution; and thus was this society kept into being and its property rescued from the sheriff's hammer. But Brother Heath only remained in the charge long enough to consummate this business, when he bade farewell to California and returned to the East, where he did efficient service for a number of years, and then went to behold the wonderful revealments of the Heavenly land.

Rev. W. S. Urmy, who at the Conference had been stationed at Alameda, was brought from that charge to take the place of Brother Heath, and fill out the balance of the year. The society now being free from debt, and the terrible cloud which had so long hovered over it and threatened its very existence having passed away, the charge at once entered upon a career of uninterrupted prosperity. In the mean time, the population in the vicinity of the

church had materially increased, and the
streets approaching it had been rendered
quite accessible by grading and sidewalk-
ing. Also several members from Powell
Street charge had moved into the neighborhood, and become identified with the work
here. Among these were Captain Goodall
and his family, whose praise has since been
in all the churches, and whose generous
deeds are constantly bringing out the true
luster of their character. The young pastor gave himself vigorously to the work,
and therefore the congregation grew, and
the spirituality of the devotional meetings
greatly increased. The year ended with
much prosperity, and the outlook was
bright indeed. At the Conference of 1857,
Brother Urmy was returned, and served
with acceptability and success during the
year. The class and prayer meetings were
exceedingly profitable, and much revival
interest prevailed. Several conversions occurred, and some were brought into the
fold at that time who remain with us till
this day. Among these are Captain Andrew Nelson and family, whose faithful
services along all these years have added
both to our material and spiritual prosperity.

At the Conference of 1858, Rev. J. A. Bruner became the pastor. He at once, by the urbanity of his manner and the sweetness of his spirit, won all hearts to himself, and gained a power for usefulness which resulted in great good to the cause. Many were the trophies won to God during that year of excessive labor and earnest toil. No people ever worked in greater harmony with their pastor, and no pastor was ever more fully imbued with intense love for perishing souls. Well do I remember how earnestly he wept between the porch and the altar, and how greatly he travailed for souls. The result was a glorious revival, which added many to the church, some of whom became the most efficient laborers that ever came within our portals. Among these were Daniel S. Howard and John Cady of precious memory, and scores of others whom I might mention. Greatly to the regret of the entire church, Brother Bruner thought that his wife's health demanded her removal from the city at the end of the year, and so his pastorate did not embrace the full constitutional term.

The Conference of 1859 gave us Rev. S. D. Simonds for our pastor. He was no stranger to the church, for he had previously lived several years in the city, and had done valiant battle for God as editor of the "California Christian Advocate" in the times that tried men's souls. So earnest was he in attacking vice through the columns of his paper, that he himself was attacked by a hired would-be assassin. The wretch's bludgeon, however, failed of executing his murderous purpose, and so the man of God was saved to exercise pastoral care over this church that had now grown into a prominent position of usefulness. Brother Simonds began and prosecuted his labors with great industry and energy, preaching, praying, and visiting from house to house incessantly, and succeeded during the two years of his pastorate in increasing quite largely the number of his personal friends and the friends of the church.

At the Conference of 1861 Rev. J. D. Blain assumed the pastorate. His appointment was an exceedingly fortunate one for the society, for he came to us determined to give us the full benefit of his great ability. This ability did not consist in wonderful pyrotechnic displays of pulpit eloquence, and yet he was eloquent; nor did it consist in massive demonstrations of logic, and yet he was logical; but it did consist in the wonderful symmetry of his character, wherein all the forces of his nature were so adjusted as to be worked to the highest degree of usefulness. He had untiring industry: time was too precious for him to squander a single moment. He had intense devotion to his work; all his thoughts centered on this. He had common practical sense to the highest degree; there was nothing visionary or unfeasible about his plans, but these were laid in the highest wisdom, and when brought to their practical working, developed into the most vital efficiency. He had the most perfect knowledge of human nature, and knew just how to touch the secret springs of every person with whom he came in contact. He was, therefore, a born leader of men. His will was indomitable, his energy unflagging. He knew no discouragement, and could brook no failure. When once his plans were settled, his impetuous nature took them up and worked them out with the resistless energy of a Niagara. He was a man of exceeding suavity of manner, insomuch that he had a kind and pleasant word for every one. He readily remembered all faces and

all names, and hence always recognized all
whom he had once seen. He was particularly careful to interest himself in strangers,
and none such came to his church without
a personal salutation from him before leaving the sanctuary. He also went from
house to house, through street and lane, in
quest of lone and homesick ones. Was it
any wonder, then, that his church at once
filled up to overflowing? Was it any marvel that seats, and aisles, and altars, and
pulpit had not space to accommodate the
crowding mass who came to his ministry?
Had such not been the case, humanity
would have been untrue to herself; for
generally is it the fact that, however degraded men or women become, however
sunken in vice or hardened in crime, kindness and sympathy will awaken in their sin-
seared hearts love and respect for the one
who bestows the boon upon them. Nor
was it surprising that the trustees, driven
by this state of facts, began to devise measures for the enlargement of their church
accommodations. This they could not do
upon their present site, and so a change of
location was forced upon their consideration. It was felt that the time had come
for Methodism in this city to take an ag-

gressive step, and plant herself in a position where she could more fully exercise the wonderful appliances of her economy for the good of men. The church, although growing and prosperous, although full of hope and courage, yet it was comparatively poor and moneyless. And while the trustees were determined on forward measures, yet the ways and means became a matter of serious question, for we had not a single rich man among us and not an advance dollar in the treasury. We had only our church property as a capital with which to begin the new enterprise. And yet so great was our necessity for larger facilities to carry on our work, and so unbounded was our confidence in the skill of our pastor to push forward the enterprise to a successful issue, that we determined to embark at once in the undertaking. Accordingly, in August, 1862, this lot was purchased at a cost of some $15,000, $8,000 of which was advanced by four brethren with which to make the first payment. Measures were inaugurated to sell our church property at once, and in a little time a purchaser was found at $8,000. This money was returned to the brethren who had made the first payment on the new lot. We also sold portions of the new lot, which gave us money enough to pay the balance that was due on its purchase. So that the case then stood that we had our present church and parsonage lot in exchange for church and lot on Folsom Street. The purchaser of our Folsom Street property insisted on having immediate possession, and so we became for a little time homeless but not friendless. The Howard Presbyterian Church were then worshiping in a small house situated on the corner of Jane and Natoma Streets, and they very generously offered us the use of their premises. This kind and fraternal offer was thankfully accepted, and our church and Sunday-school services were transferred to that temple.

Meanwhile, the parsonage was removed from the old lot to the new, and the work of erecting this church commenced. So limited were our means and so small our resources, that we at first determined to let contracts only for the basement. The brickwork was assigned to Brother E. B. Sammis, and the carpenter-work to Brother James Harlow; both of whom belonged to the Board of Trustees, and therefore had more than a selfish interest in the enterprise. These brethren were faithful to their trusts, and worked with great vigor and dispatch, so that not many weeks elapsed before the basement was ready for occupancy. It was covered over with a temporary asphaltum roof, and our Israel removed the Ark of the Lord within its walls. To connect the old with the new, the seats from the old church were brought down and placed in position, and served a useful purpose in the basement, until the Central Church was built, when they were transferred to that house, and thus gave ocular demonstration of their itinerant proclivities. During all these weeks, the pastor had not been idle; for in addition to performing all his pulpit and pastoral duties, he was incessant in soliciting and collecting money to carry on the enterprise, and so successful was he in this department, that no laborer on this temple ever went an hour unpaid when his money was due. Having now a commodious and comfortable basement to winter in, we rested from our material labors, and gave ourselves more fully to the spiritual services of the church. The winter was passed with much profit to the people, as all the services were most intensely interesting. Sinners were converted, and saints were greatly strength-

ened and built up in holiness and godly
living. A constant baptism from the excellent glory rested upon all who came within
our borders, and a divine afflatus filled the
temple continually. We needed no further
demonstration that our offering was accepted, and that our enterprise had won the
divine approval; and so it was determined
that when the spring had opened and the
rains ceased, the enterprise should be
pushed to its completion. Our pastor
nerved himself to the task, and resumed the
work of soliciting funds; and many a weary
day did he tramp these streets, and many a
night did he return to the parsonage footsore and worn, but not discouraged. The
Board of Trustees stood nobly by his side,
and held nightly sessions, lasting often till
midnight, in devising schemes and suggesting plans for the advancement of the work;
and so we builded the walls, working in
great harmony and with great heart, until
all was completed. And then the ladies
undertook the work of upholstering and
furnishing, and magnificently did they succeed. Herculean work did they perform,
insomuch that at one fair at Platt's Hall
they made over $5,000 for the treasury.

The temple was dedicated on the 18th of

October, 1863, Rev. Dr. J. T. Peek preaching the sermon; but the joyfulness of the occasion was marred by the knowledge that one, who had been most active and efficient in promoting the enterprise, lay bleeding and dying at his home, and could not mingle in the services of the hour. Daniel S. Howard, one of the trustees, who had given his time and money and wonderful energy, from the moment the scheme was inaugurated till the finishing touch was given the edifice, had but a day or two before met with a fearful accident through a runaway horse, by which both legs were broken, and the nervous system so shocked that death resulted October 20th, 1863. We brought his precious remains to this altar, and his was the first funeral eulogy pronounced from this desk. Sad, indeed, that it so soon should be consecrated to such service! But Brother Howard was ready; Oh, how ready! He had been steadily growing in grace, becoming sweeter and purer in spirit, receiving greater manifestations of divine glory, for the entire year preceding his death; and when the sudden call came, he simply responded, " Yes, Lord Jesus, I come quickly." Twenty years have flown since that time, but his name is green and fresh in the memory of his associates of that day, and it cannot fade from the records of this church while a brick or stone of the temple remains. Nor will his work then cease, for the results of his earthly labor can only be gathered when the harvest is garnered in the skies.

Another of the trustees who had been specially active in the promotion of the work, and had in fact been the master builder of these foundations and walls till the topmost stone was reached, Edward B. Sammis, was attacked with bronchitis and hemorrhage of the lungs, and was compelled to leave the coast and return to his home in Brooklyn, New York, just before the dedication took place. He lingered for a few months after his arrival there, hovering on the brink of death's dark river, when the seething billows arose and swept him into that world beyond the flood, where the temple is already built and the laborers are at rest. Our love for this peerless man was so great, and our respect for him so profound, that a special minute was made on the records of the Board, regretting his departure and conveying to him our most tender sympathy and Christian regards. But a higher record has been made of his glorious deeds, and his name is all glittering with golden light as it stands upon the foremost page of the Lamb's Book of Life.

Nor should we fail to mention other names whose owners were conspicuous in their labors for the interests of the church. Such men as Frederick A. Beardsley, James Harlow, and Samuel S. Sprague were ever ready to aid in the promotion of its welfare, nor did their attachment cease till the Master beckoned them to the skies. They were exceedingly efficient in that department of the work that each was best fitted for. Harlow was wise in counsel as to all mechanical matters, Sprague earnest and untiring in collecting church revenues, Beardsley always on the alert to advance church interests in whatever form possible. And so they labored in the Master's vineyard till the evening hour came, when they quit the field of toil for the sweet rest of heaven. We mournfully laid their ashes in earth's last receptacle, where they await the reconstruction touch of the resurrection morn, when they shall rise, fashioned after the similitude of Christ's glorious body.

The Conference came which ended Brother Blain's constitutional term before the church was dedicated, and it was agreed that the charge should be left to be supplied, and Brother Blain take a supernumerary relation without an appointment, so that he might act as the supply under the appointment of the Presiding Elder. In this way he remained the pastor of the church for the third year. This was thought indispensable to the safety of the enterprise, inasmuch as there were many unpaid subscriptions that he only could collect. At the dedication all bills were brought in, and the whole account was made up. It was found that we had expended some $65,000, $14,000 of which we still owed. The people had done so nobly that we had no heart to press them further for money, and so we concluded to carry this debt till the money forces of the church had recuperated sufficiently to warrant another effort being made. So the money was borrowed—$10,000 on mortgage, and $4,000 on the trustees' note—and all bills were fully paid. Being treasurer of the Board through the whole enterprise, and knowing whereof I affirm, I can truthfully say that no banking institution ever met its obligations with more promptitude than did the trustees of this church during all its building operations; nor was there any moneyed institution in the city that had a better credit than it for the amount it needed to borrow.

Relieved of this intense money strain, Brother Blain now gave himself fully to the pulpit and the pastorate, preaching with great acceptability, and leading on the host with large success. He retained his hold on the affections of the people up to the last of his ministry in the charge.

During the last year of Brother Blain's administration measures were taken to inaugurate a new church to the westward, whither a large population had settled. The Howard Street Board accordingly leased a lot on the south side of Mission Street, between Sixth and Seventh, and built a chapel thereon for Sunday-school and church purposes. A Sunday-school was at once organized and officered from members of our own church, and James F. Smith was its first superintendent. He was assisted by a corps of as earnest Sunday-school workers as ever engaged in that most laudable enterprise, and it was not long before they had gathered into the school from the surrounding community a large number of scholars, so that scarcely a year of existence had elapsed before the school numbered its hundreds of intensely interested and earnest workers. At the Conference of 1864, the enterprise shaped into a church organization, and took the name of the Central M. E. Church of San Francisco, and Brother Blain was appointed its pastor. We gave to this enterprise some fifty of our membership, and a large share of financial and sympathetic aid. In fact, it was our own child, and why should we not cherish and nourish it till its own strength should allow it to go alone? That branch has since grown into a strong and sturdy tree, and is now producing abundant fruit to the glory of God. Of course, to reach its present state of prosperous usefulness, it has had many severe struggles, but its brave and sturdy ones have undauntedly carried the work forward with true Christian heroism and great self-denial.

Just before the lease expired to the Mission Street lot, the northeast corner of Sixth and Minna Streets was purchased for its permanent habitation, and the chapel was moved to this lot. It was a magnificent selection, as the lot was eighty feet front and one hundred feet deep, and being on a corner afforded very fine lighting facilities. Its frontage was also on a prospective business street, and needed only time to develop into a magnificent property, which should not only form ample church accommodations for the society above, but also afford a grand opportunity to line its front below with a row of stores, whose revenue for all time could have been used for church extension or other evangelizing movements. But, as is generally the case with church enterprises, the society was too poor to wait for this surely coming financial opportunity, and so the lot was sold for the same amount that it cost, and its present site was purchased for a smaller price, and the little chapel again put on wheels and removed to the new purchase. Here it remained till the present edifice supplanted it. And so has this society moved onward and upward in the increase of its church appliances, and the magnitude of its glorious career of human elevation and human salvation. And so has the Howard Street Church supplemented its own direct efforts by the wonderfully energized industry of this its most queenly daughter. And who can tell the magnitude of its usefulness by founding this new evangelizing agency? None till the books are opened at the last assize, when the sum of human weal and woe shall be revealed.

Among those who greatly aided us in this work were some outside friends—outside so far as actual church membership is concerned, but outside in no other sense, for they were in the congregation as regularly as any of us; they were also at all social and devotional meetings of the church; yea, they were members of the Board of Trustees, and participated most fully in all our plans for our material advancement. They were foremost in the extent of their subscriptions, and lavish in the fullness of their contributions. And so did William H. Gawley labor in the outer court to build the temple. And so did Robert G. Bixby furnish a large share of counsel and of cash. And in later time William H. Howland gave us much valuable aid. These names will remain emblazoned upon our record as those who evinced by their noble acts a great love for our Methodist nation, and a great disposition to assist in building us a sanctuary.

The Conference of 1864 gave us Rev. Dr. J. T. Peck for our pastor. His first year was quite successful, and resulted in cancelling the floating debt of $4,000. It also added to the church over one hundred probationers as the result of a gracious revival. He was reappointed in 1865, but did not remain in the charge more than half the year, his wife's health necessitating his return to the East. After his departure, the church was placed in my charge, and the pulpit was mostly supplied with what ministerial help we could conveniently secure. The social meetings were well attended, and the spirituality and profitableness of those meetings were matter of universal comment. During this year the organ was purchased and placed in the gallery, at a cost of some $2,500. But the money was not raised to pay for it, and therefore the debt was increased by that amount.

After the departure of Dr. Peck, it was thought by some that the salvation of the church depended upon the importation from the East of some distinguished Doctor of Divinity, who should be able to cope with the giant evils of this coast, and so a committee of correspondence was appointed by the Board. One of our trustees was going East at that time, and he was requested to visit the centers of population and see what could be done. Suffice it to say, that after much correspondence with various parties, the Bishop took the matter in his own hands and sent us one whom we had no previous thought of. And so at the Conference of 1866, Rev. Dr. Cox was announced as our pastor. He met with a warm reception on the part of the church, and was awarded a larger salary than any man who had previously served this people. He entered upon his labors with much vigor, and prosecuted them with great industry and success. His prayer meetings soon became the rallying point of Israel's hosts, and the lecture-room was thronged to its utmost capacity at every weekly meeting. He remained in the charge three years, and during that time increased the membership largely, added the basement to the parsonage, paid the entire debt that existed when he came, both funded and floating, frescoed the walls of the auditorium, and filled the windows with stained glass, so dark that one on entering the edifice imagines it more a Mausoleum than a Christian temple, where the light of the living God is shining.

In 1869 Dr. Cox was succeeded by Rev. L. Walker, a young man of brilliant parts, so far as his intellectual status was concerned. He continued to do efficient service in the charge for two years and a half, when he was turned aside from his appropriate work by his love for fast horses and financial speculations, and so was his power for usefulness blasted and his ministerial life made a wreck. His stranded bark lies beached on the sands of time, a fearful warning to those who would come down from the lofty pinnacle of the Christian ministry to toy with the world's baubles. During the last half of the third year of Mr. Walker's term we were again left without a pastor. The working force of the church, however, had now gained such completeness of discipline and such strength of labor that no material damage came of the deprivation. The tribes of our Israel went on with the battle against sin and her cohorts, with only the Lion of the tribe of Judah as our leader, and the Lord of hosts was with us, and the God of Jacob was our refuge. Prayer and class meetings were well attended, and the people grew mightily in the fellowship of the Spirit and the comfort of the Holy Ghost. The Word was preached by invited guests, and so the pulpit was made attractive by variety. Meanwhile, our former pastor, Rev. Dr. Peck, who had now become one of the Bishops of the church, was looking sharply for a man who should be fully furnished in all respects to be an ensample to the flock. He was stimulated in this service, not merely by an impulse to do his duty as a general superintendent of the church, but by the great special love he bore this people. He was, therefore, the more intensely solicitous that no mistake be made in the selection that had been confided to his hands.

We trusted him and were not disappointed, for at the Conference of 1872 Rev. Frank F. Jewell was announced as the chosen leader. He came to us in the vigor of robust physical health, and in the fullness of the gospel of peace. At once all the appliances of the church felt the spring of a new enthusiasm, and all departments of our Zion bounded into more intense activity. Crowds began to throng our aisles, and sacred fire burned upon our altars. The three years of his sojourn were years of ever-increasing prosperity to this Zion, wherein both the material and spiritual interests of the church were wondrously advanced. Ten thousand dollars' worth of improvements had been added to the property in a new organ-loft, and certain changes in basement and Sunday-school room. This amount, together with the previously accrued debt of $4-

000, made us again in need of $14,000. The whole amount was generously subscribed, but for the want of sufficient vigor on the part of the collectors, some of it remained unpaid, and so about $3,500 debt was carried over to the next pastorate. Dr. Jewell left the charge under a full tide of prosperity, his congregations filling every nook and cranny of this spacious auditorium even up to the hour of his departure.

The Rev. Thomas Guard came to us in 1875. Long before his arrival his great reputation as a pulpit orator had reached us, and public expectation was on the *qui vive*. He had previously occupied the pulpit of the finest church in American Methodism, and his fame was in all thoughts and on every tongue. We need not deny that we, as a people, felt some vainglory in having such a star—nay, such a sun to shed its refulgence athwart our way. We were not a little surprised when he came, to find him the simple, childlike man that he was, for his was a nature of the finest sensibility and most guileless character. Like a nicely attuned instrument is adjusted to the most exquisite harmony, so every fiber of his being thrilled and teemed with eloquence. And then

this was not so much the eloquence of rosy
words as the beautiful and forceful expression
of most massive and sublime thoughts.
But Dr. Guard lived in too high a sphere,
moved in too vast a mental and spiritual
realm, to be thoroughly appreciated by this
sordid, muckrake-loving world. His was
not, therefore, a ministry of every-day
practical life, but was one of great ideal
beauty to those who could follow him in
his flights of fancy, or linger with him on
those supernal cliffs whither his peerless
imagination continually soared. And so
during the three years of his ministry, the
people were instructed and delighted rather
than that the material interests of the
charge were advanced. Money was too
material for such an administration, and
yet money was a desideratum, and had to
come, if not from legitimate resources, still
come it must even from the Shylock's coffers.
So this edifice was again mortgaged, and
we were again within the iron grip of the
interest-gatherers.

The Conference of 1878 sent back the
first pastor again, and Rev. M. C. Briggs,
D. D., was once more installed. When he
taught us the way of life some twenty-six
years before, he was only plain Brother

Briggs, as Doctors of Divinity were unknown to California Methodism then. But now the D. D. came with him, and we stood in awe of it, but we soon learned how little titles affect character, after all, and were not long in realizing that the same Brother Briggs of other years was here—here to preach the same old gospel of the grace of God, here to tell the old, old story of redeeming love, here to pray and sing and shout and crowd on the column of the Lord's advancing host. His three years were years of incessant labor and vigorous toil. Well done will the Master say when the reckoning comes.

Brother Jewell was returned to us in 1881. The first year of his present term resulted in a great ingathering of souls through the assistance of that wonderfully efficient evangelist, Rev. Thomas Harrison, and the refurnishing and replenishing of the church throughout, at an expenditure of some $3,000; all of which was paid when the work was done. This second year of his administration has canceled the entire debt of the church, and we are once more free from the death-grip of the mortgage. We surely have cause for gratitude, and do rejoice most heartily that our year of jubilee has fully come.

And now, had we such power of discernment as would enable us to look back along the track of all these years, and gather up the results of all this labor; could we take in the good that has been done and the evil that has been prevented; could we see the tide of life that has been invoked and the torrent of death that has been stayed; could we realize the number of hearts that have been comforted, the number of brightest hopes that have been inspired, the number of straying feet that have been turned from the broad to the narrow way; could we know the extent and power of influence that has been exerted on the public sentiment of this community during all these years of strange and stirring history—we would then be thoroughly furnished with factors sufficient to solve the problem, whether this labor has been in vain, and whether the organization of this society was not an event of the most stupendous magnitude. Nay, more; could we look out on the on-coming ages, and behold the future of this church in the scope of its evangelizing movements along all those revolving cycles, until the millennium shall dawn; could we see the trophies it shall win, the laurels it shall bind on human-

uel's brow, the victory on victory that shall be inscribed on its banner as it floats grandly in the midst of all moral conflicts— yea, could we go further and push our raptured gaze beyond the confines of time into the vast mysteries of eternity; could we look into the holy city where the many mansions be, and where the white-robed throng is before the throne; could we listen to the harpers harp and the chanters chant; could we gaze on the bespangled multitude which no man can number, and behold among those shining ranks those who have gone up from our midst, and who were our companions in labor and sacrifice; could we see hundreds upon hundreds who were converted at our altars, and sanctified in the midst of our solemn feasts; could we behold them there so free from sin, so filled with rapturous delight, so safe forevermore in the presence of him who redeemed them and made them joint-heirs with himself to the inheritance of the skies—we would then have some faint idea of the grandeur of our investment and the magnificent outcome of our toil. Nor would we fail to realize the immensity of that glorious sea of results which began in the trickling rill of 1851, and, thrilled by the rapturous vision, in the fullness of our joy would we exclaim, "Halleluiah, for the Lord God has done wonderful things for our Zion."

SENECA JONES.
First Superintendent Sunday School.

PASTORAL REMINISCENCES.

A vast congregation assembled at the church in the evening to continue the Jubilee services. The interest was intense and the services extremely entertaining, as several former pastors were present, who would convey to the audience something of the days of Auld Lang Syne. First among these was introduced the Rev. D. A. Dryden, who said:

My pastorate in connection with this church, over a quarter of a century ago, when it was known as the Folsom St. Church, was a brief one. I shall claim the privilege of making my remarks correspondingly brief. The inner-heart history of this church during that time will never be written. It was anything but a time of jubilee. It was a struggle for life rather than a time of triumph; there was more of Gethsemane than of the Mount of Transfiguration. Like individuals, churches have their birth, childhood, and maturer growth. Like individuals, some are born healthy and strong, with all the potencies of a rapid, vigorous growth, and sturdy maturity, and favored with all the conditions of such growth. Such Folsom St. Church was not. It was born feeble—some thought prematurely—had a sickly childhood, environed by adverse conditions which often threatened to cut short its career. During the year 1855 was perhaps the severest struggle for life, at least it was severe enough. Congregations were very small, membership few, rather poor. Income from every available source sadly below even the most rigidly economical expenses; crushed down under a heavy debt, with constantly accumulating interest. The heart struggles of pastor and a few noble souls are known only to the Good Master. Surely there were no visible signs then of the powerful manhood into which the feeble child has grown. And who knoweth to what extent, under the brooding providence of God, the baptism of these days of trial may have contributed to this growth? Not always in prosperity does life take its deepest roots, either in the church or the individual.

In looking back, even from this night of jubilee, I can realize it was a privilege to have had a share in those adversities, perhaps realize it more now than then; for in truth the old Adam in me did not so much consider it a privilege then.

In one important respect this church has been specially blessed. During all its years of feebleness and struggle it has had nursing fathers and mothers who have never despaired or abandoned their child. Such was John D. Blain, whose memory is fresh with all of us to-day. As Presiding Elder at that time, I do remember well how I was nerved to new endeavor by the magic power of his cheerful courage, and unflagging zeal and energy. For every desperate extremity he seemed to evolve some new expedient. But I believe that, under God, the church owes its continued existence and growth to present robust maturity to the persistent faith and persevering endeavor of a few noble men and women, some of whom I could name. A venerable few are here to-night, who have stood by their church through all its vicissitudes from the cradle to its present prosperous surroundings: surely they have a right to a full cup of rejoicing in this jubilee. Others, too, I could name who are not here in bodily presence. They have passed over and entered the New Jerusalem. But I have felt

to-day that they could turn aside a little,
even from the glories of the church triumphant, to be present in spirit with us
here.

Rev. W. S. Urmy said:

It is very gratifying to meet with you
on this happy occasion, and I sincerely congratulate you on being free from the heavy
burden which, as a church, you have been
so long bearing. It was my pleasure to
serve some of you, with others who have
gone joyously on before to the better land,
many years ago, and the memories of those
days are full of interest; but as the time is
limited, it will be possible to mention but a
few of the facts and incidents of my too
short pastorate over this society.

I arrived in California on the 16th of
August, 1853—nearly thirty years ago, and
the first service I attended in San Francisco
was held in Music Hall on Bush street near
Montgomery—the temporary home at that
time of this congregation. The sermon
was by Bro. N. P. Heath, who was then
serving his first term with you. I remember a little after attending a Sunday school
held in a school-house, in what was then
called Happy Valley, the school-house being then somewhere near what is now the

corner of Mission and Second streets. This
visit was in company with Bro. W. H. Coddington, who was then, I think, superintendent, and who afterward served in that
capacity with much acceptability and success during my pastorate, and for many
years besides.

I joined the Conference in February, 1854,
and was first appointed to Coloma, where
gold was first discovered; then to Columbia
and Sonora, in company with J. W. Brier;
then to Ione, and in 1856 to Alameda, with
Bro. Chas. H. Northup as my colleague.
While preaching there the work was divided, Bro. Northup taking the southern part
of the work, leaving me to fill Alameda and
Clinton, or what is now East Oakland. At
that time Bro. D. Deal was at the Bethel;
his brother, Dr. W. Grove Deal being in
charge of the school at Alameda. Bro.
Deal wished that I should be changed from
Alameda to the Bethel, so that he might
fill Alameda and thus assist in the school.
But Bro. Blain, who was then Presiding
Elder, wished to place me at Folsom street;
Bro. Heath, who was filling his second term
in this charge, having become discouraged
and intending to leave.

One Monday morning, in March, 1857,

there were a number of preachers in the *Advocate* office, which was then on Clay street. Bro. Deal was urging Bro. Blain to place me at the Bethel, and Bro. Blain objected to this, and said: "I want you to go to Folsom street." I think I said, "Well," and thus my appointment was fixed, and on the next week I went to work.

The members of the church were much discouraged; though the debt, which was much more burdensome than the one you have just so wisely paid, had been removed by aid of a large missionary appropriation. There was a proposition really entertained to sell the church for school purposes and disband; but we tried to look on the bright side of things and build up the cause, and the members taking hold with a will, we were soon out of the trough of the sea, and then had plain and pleasant sailing.

Some thought I was quite a young man to be placed in so responsible a position, and good Bro. Burns, of Powell Street Church, said to me one morning, at Allen & Spier's store, in a joking manner, "Go ahead now, Bro. Urmy, and beat Dr. Scott." The sarcasm of the remark received point from the fact that the Doctor was then at the height of his fame as pastor of Calvary

Church, then situated on Bush street, just below Montgomery.

The prayer-meetings increased in interest and in the number attending, and from thirteen, which we thought a good number, we soon went up to thirty or more. The class-meetings also became seasons of great spiritual profit, and it was necessary to have three or four where before one answered.

At one of the prayer-meetings an incident occurred of rather a startling nature. Bro. McPhun, who then lived on First street, had come to the meeting with his wife, leaving the children at home, the residence being back of a small store which they then kept. When the meeting was about half through the door opened, and Bro. McPhun, turning round, started up in affright, and making the exclamation, "Holy Mother," commenced to walk over the pews back of him. I looked toward the door, and saw a child coming in crying, and with its night dress all covered with blood. The meeting suddenly closed. It seems the children had supposed some one was about entering the house, and going to the front door had found it locked. In endeavoring to break through the window this one had cut itself quite badly, though not fatally.

Member after member now joined and some were soundly converted, among them Bros. Nelson and Peterson. The Sunday school increased in size and interest; improvements were made, a brick wall being built in front of the lot and a sidewalk laid. The exterior of the building was painted, and the interior whitened; and from that time, for several reasons, the prosperity of the charge was insured; the principal factor in the success being the firmness and persistence of the members, the living part of whom it may not be permissible for me to personally refer to, but it will not be out of place for me to mention Sammis and Beardsley and Howard and Sisters Augusta Townsend and Stringer, and others of precious memory, who so nobly toiled and paid and attended with right royal perseverance, until a success was assured which we are now enjoying the results of, and the future outcome of which no man can imagine.

Capt. Charles Goodall said:

When this church was built there were in a very marked degree four characteristics shown in a single individual, viz.: *piety, wisdom, energy,* and *perseverance.* The individual possessing these four desirable qualifications for such a work was the Rev. J. D. Blain.

The first—piety—meaning obedient love of the will of God, and *zealous devotion* to his service.

If I am any judge, after knowing a man intimately in sunshine and storm, in sickness and health, in prosperity and adversity, as I did know Brother Blain, he was entirely devoted to whatever he thought was the will of his Maker; and no matter what it cost him if he saw it was his duty, he was sure to do it.

The second—wisdom—which we understand to be the use of the best means to attain the best ends. This was shown in his management of the business of disposing of the old property and securing the new.

Third—energy—the capacity and will to pursue in a strong and vigorous manner whatever his duty called him to.

He was strong and vigorous, both in body and mind, and full of the resources of good health, common sense, keen and clear of *intellect*, a true embodiment of a Christian, and *every inch a man*.

Fourth — perseverance — continued pursuit or prosecution of any business or enterprise begun.

After the decision of himself and officiary, he left no stone unturned.

Going from house to house, merchant to merchant, business man to business man, mechanic to mechanic, and all trades, avocations and callings that could be reached. Rebuffs abashed him not; he would be heard, and generally accomplished his object.

He thought it was just as much serving God and preaching, with the plan of the church in his hand and arguing for a subscription, as it was to be in the pulpit with the Bible before him explaining and elucidating the scriptures.

It enabled him to make personal application to individuals, which was his strong forte. He would not be put off; where others would be bluffed off in dismay, he would come off triumphant with a subscription.

Besides these virtues that characterized the Pastor, there were in the official Board and membership, a faith in the result, and a unity of action that was begotten thereby, and that was a harbinger of final triumph.

Tug of war—up guards, and at them.

It is said, separate the atoms which make the *hammer*, and each would fall on the stone as a snowflake; weld it together, and wielded by the firm arm of the quarry man, it will break the massive rocks asunder.

Divide the waters of Niagara into distinct and individual drops, and they will be no more than the falling rain; but in their united body they would quench the fires of Versuvius, and have some to spare for the volcanos of other mountains.

But he has gone and they have gone. The strong and manly bodies of Blain, Sammis, Howard, Harlow, Beardsley, Gawley, and Sprague, of them that helped to build up this edifice, are no more on earth: they have gone, as have also Peck and Guard, the learned and eloquent preachers whose efforts we shall always remember. Six trustees and three preachers have gone to join the innumerable company which no man can number; they have washed their robes and made them white in the blood of the Lamb.

To-day they see and know what we are doing; they join in joyous jubilee as we raise it here: it is answered and echoed in heaven; we cannot hear their voices (except in memory), but they can hear ours. If we live and die as they did (and I have faith to think we shall), we shall join with them.

"We shall meet, we shall sing, we shall reign
  In the land where the saved never die;
 We shall rest free from sorrow and pain
  With them in the sweet bye and bye."

Rev. J. A. Bruner said:

I remember that on a certain Thursday night, October, 1858, with wife and children, landing from the Sacramento steamer, we were met by representative men of the charge, Wm. H. Coddington, R. McElroy, and Capt. Charles Goodall, who for three successive nights had been awaiting our arrival at the wharf. We were hospitably entertained at the home of Capt. Goodall until the parsonage was ready for occupancy.

Though strangers to all, our reception was hearty, and our intercourse with the society and congregation cordial without exception during our stay.

Entering into the labors of my faithful predecessor, Rev. W. S. Urmy, I found an appreciative people prepared of the Lord.

Our official meetings were earnest, brotherly, harmonious; no overshadowing power dictating the *regimen*; we all strove together in love.

Every man was loyal to the interests of the charge, ready to do, willing to work and to contribute.

A noticeable feature of the society was its social atmosphere, more apt to be found in small churches, where each and all may have recognition and brotherly attention; where equality largely prevails, and a common interest unites hearts and hands in earnest church work.

My new little study in the rear of the church, a part of the parsonage, was comfortable, quiet, shut in from the bustle and noise of the city. It also accommodated business meetings and class services, which were earnest, spiritual, and well sustained.

From a brief journal kept at the time, I am able to sketch some of the facts of spiritual life and progress at that time.

Dec. 15th, 1858. At our Wednesday night prayer meeting, towards its close, Hiram R—— an interesting young man, came unsolicited, and kneeling at the altar gave God his heart, and became a new creature in Christ Jesus.

The following Sunday this young man spoke excellently in class, saying: "This Sabbath is worth more to me than all the days of my past life."

Jan. 19th, 1859. God has, in answer to prayer, begun a gracious work in my charge. The society is striving after a closer walk with God.

Last week a young man entered into perfect love. This week a sister who had lost the blessing of purity many years ago in Maine, had it restored. She seems the most active member of the charge.

Every evening professors and penitents kneel at the altar for pardon or purity. Last night two men found Jesus, and publicly acknowledged the gift of God. One of them is our organist. May the gracious work deepen and extend.

Jan. 23rd, Sunday morning. On Thursday and Friday evenings, from ten to thirteen presented themselves as seekers of pardon. Satan strove hard to baffle, but both evenings the Lord saved souls. Some six or eight have found peace.

Jan. 24th, Monday. Yesterday my faith claimed the promises in behalf of God's work in our midst, and it was honored.

Jan. 28th. At no time since coming to the State have I felt such yearnings for sinners. Yesterday my heart was much drawn out in prayer and tender regard for souls.

Last night, after a short sermon by Bro. Thomas, a filled altar attested the fact of a deepening and widening of the work.

Jan. 29th. To-night Dr. Peck preached to a large audience, the altar was filled, several found peace, and six offered for probation.

Jan. 30th. This morning I was enabled to press the subject of a present salvation. After sermon Bro. E. Thomas consecrated the elements for and assisted in our first monthly communion. Some who lately found the Savior were deeply affected.

In the afternoon at the Sunday School, before the opening prayer, I asked "how many children and youth desire remembrance in prayer?" A number of young ladies and many of the children rose. Twenty adults were present in my Bible Class, some of whom were lately converted.

Wednesday and Friday, 9th and 11th Feb., were observed as days of fasting and prayer for extension of the work.

Sunday, 13th Feb., baptised four young men, and received four young men into full membership.

At close of sermon the whole congregation knelt in silent prayer.

Bro. R. McElroy then concluded with appropriate petitions.

The presiding Elder, Rev. M. C. Briggs, called with me to see our well attended Sunday school. At close of evening service all except two persons remained for the prayer meeting.

Feb. 19th, Saturday afternoon, forty persons present at 2 o'clock, to hear Bro. Briggs' first sermon at our second quarterly meeting.

The next morning at 9 o'clock held Love-feast. The scene was thrilling, in part from the number of nationalities represented in a company of perhaps less than one hundred.

The story of salvation was told, not only by Americans, but subjects of the British crown from the Provinces, from London, various parts of Great Britain; men from Germany, Sweden, Norway, Denmark; the Russian from St. Petersburg; the darker Spaniard from Malaga, each and all spoke the language of Canaan and rejoiced together in Christ Jesus. The occasion will never be forgotten. Some of those who testified that day to the power of saving grace have long since passed to their heavenly home. Among the number, Capt. Daniel S. Howard, who gave his heart to God in our midst during the revival, was a power for good in every department of the church; a burning and shining light, until years afterward he was suddenly called to his heavenly rest.

So also, the venerable Cady, who so heartily embraced the great salvation, and as a patriarch exemplifying the spirit of his divine Master, until several years since he was not, for God took him.

The following entry in my journal indicates the progress and results of the work up to that date:

Feb. 25th. Six weeks since I began a series of meetings in my charge which have continued every evening until the present.

About 20 persons or upwards have professed conversion, the principle part of whom within the first two weeks. Also, some 12 or 14 joined by letter, which increased the society of Folsom street charge from 70 to 100 or more. The Sunday school has also doubled.

I have said that the charge were ready and willing workers. The benefactions of the church were all represented at the close of the year.

On Sunday morning, July 31st, after a sermon by Bishop Baker, in less than 15 minutes we raised $600—being in full of all indebtedness for parsonage, improvements, etc.

The following contains the last memoranda from my journal of that year:

Aug. 7, 1859. Held our fourth quarterly meeting. Rev. M. C. Briggs preached morning and evening, and administered the Lord's Supper.

During the year not one of our number have died; no one been expelled; no church trial; no complaint; no appeal. The Lord be praised!

Such is, in brief, a sketch of my happy twelve months' pastorate with this loving people; at the close of which against their earnest protest I felt it duty, for the sake of the health of my family, to occupy a new field of labor. How swiftly those years have sped away! Though a goodly proportion of the old Folsom street membership continue, a new generation has grown up around them; another house of worship, spacious, commodious, contains the largely increased society and congregation; hundreds of new Sunday school scholars attend the exercises of faithful teachers, and join in glad hosannas to the Great Head of the church.

Rev. S. D. Simonds said:

I suppose that in these Jubilee services some personal references are expected. In common with most ministers and all thoughtful men, in all ages, I have deeply pondered the question of human responsibility. I came early to the conclusion that the universal law for each, man or woman, was to do all the good which the environments of each rendered possible to be done. To do good of every possible sort, both to the bodies and souls of men, is the life of religion. Without this all piety is pretense; all faith but the faith of devils.

This sense of responsibility led me to the Christian ministry, and as far as possible with my surroundings kept me in it to the present. The Christian ministry, however the declaration may excite surprise in the minds of mere naturalists, is the greatest source of blessing to the world. Unless the light of spiritual truth and the affection of goodness and purity be in the mind, there is no power of self-help with man.

> It takes a soul
> To move a body. * *
> It takes the ideal to blow a hair's breath off
> The dust of the actual. * * *
> Life develops from within.

I have had the largest sympathy with reformers, so called, but who has not marked their distressing failures. Reformers generally have the greatest need to be reformed. Their shadow goes backward and not forward on the dial of progress.

The fact is, nothing in this world grows except from seed. And the seed of human growth is the word made flesh, then glorified, or made spirit and life. That word preached unto men brings divine light and divine love into the human soul as an organizing force, and renders all progress possible, and great progress in civilization certain. Soon the German nation will celebrate the four-hundredth anniversary of the birthday of Martin Luther. Well and nobly should it be done; for Martin Luther gave them the Bible in German, which has done more for the nation than all her needle and Krupp guns. And its light is but just dawning. It will go on blessing the land while time shall last. Similar has been the power of the English Bible to advance and bless the English and American peoples. The word is the cloud by day and the pillar of fire by night by which the modern Israel of all humanity journeys to a glorious Canaan of a perfect civilization, and each obedient soul comes to glory. The negations of unbelief and the dark tyrannies of service are but eddies in the stream, and parts of the onward movement before it is understood.

It was my most earnest effort for years to promote the spiritual life of the people. I never speculated. I never lost myself in forms. I tried to avoid beating the air with common-place expression. If I was not understood by others—for rarely is advancing thought accepted at once—I understood myself to herald forth the light of the new day on which I felt the world had entered. And yet it was the Old World interpreted by the demonstrations of experience, and in the light of that spirit which was promised to guide into all truth. If the Lord Jesus said more than eighteen hundred years ago, "I have many things to say unto you, but ye cannot bear them now," was it not time to walk in the light of the Holy Comforter, even the Spirit of truth?

Let your minds glance over the two great dispensations, the Mosaic and the Christian: the first, intensely external and natural; the second, natural with inspirations of the Spirit. Both equally divine, but one of law, the other of grace and truth. Walk along the track of history to the eighteenth century. Has the Kingdom of God come? The churches, whether Greek, Roman or Protestant, are altogether external; no more the Kingdom of God than the Empire of Charlemagne, Charles V. or Napoleon I. The prophetic periods are closed. No man carefully governed by Scripture can carry the prophetic periods beyond 1830, if he can later than 1750. After thirteen years of very intense and careful study of prophecy, I could find no point below 1730, or thereabout. I was utterly at sea, and could not accept the theories that brought the world to an end in 1843. It ought to have ended before.

But let us look at God's commentary in Providence on his word. In 1729, Mr. Wesley organized his societies. It was not the first perception of a spiritual kingdom. The United Brethren and the Quakers existed already. But it was the clearest, simplest, and most powerful organization for spiritual truth that the world had seen. And the doctrine of the witness of the Spirit to the word of God was clearly announced.

Such a phenomenon I call a new dispensation of Christian truth and life. If the dogmas of the sixteenth century have been foisted upon it; if the ecclesiasticisms of the middle ages have laid their hands upon it in any degree; they no more belong to it than the Judaism of the old Pharisees belongs to Christianity. Methodism must cast them off, or God will raise another people to take her crown. Her mission is to hold forth God's written word, and proclaim the demonstration of its truth in the hearts and lives of believers, a living faith a living, supernatural (higher nature) religion, the kingdom of God in men, which though small in its beginnings, will advance more and more forever. We are but in the dawn of the spiritual church, where the Lord Jesus is the all in all. I sought to promote, as far as I was able, while pastor of this church, the spiritual life of the people. I made no effort to preach eloquent or learned sermons : but I love eloquence and learning, and honor them every where; but I was so intent on the spirit of regeneration among men, that I had no time to polish periods, or shape the climax with declamation. It was to make Christ known as the resurrection and the life, that filled the measure of my ambition. I felt that if I could plant spirituality in the people, it would be the greatest good to them, and the greatest good to the world, and lay the broadest foundation for the prosperity of the church. I hope it is not with any vanity in my heart that I survey the past, in the confident belief that to the spiritual life then infused into the people, this church owes more of its prosperity than to any man or set of men. Such prosperity is not my honor. It is the honor of God, to whom be all glory forever—Amen.

PEN PICTURES.

BY ROBERT MC ELROY.

HAD RESPECT UNTO THE RECOMPENSE.

One evening, in the early part of 1862, a young man came into our prayer meeting and took a seat near the altar. His personal appearance was prepossessing and his manner exceedingly devout. His face beamed with a heavenly radiancy, and his eye sparkled with the fire of pure devotion. His voice was clear and ringing, and when engaged in prayer, exhortation or song, seemed to melt all present into the most exquisite tenderness. He talked so eloquently of the love of Jesus; he pleaded so prevailingly at the throne of grace; he sung, O! how sweetly, of that home where the glorified rest from life's weary toil. All eyes were upon him and all hearts were stirred to their profoundest depths by the magic of his manner and the exceeding sweetness of his religious exercises. Wonder who he is and whence he came? Such was the curious inquiry which came leaping from all lips, and yet none seemed able to answer the inquiry or satisfy the curiosity. There he was, stranger to all, and yet all hearts thrilling under the pathos and power of his devotions. Like the risen Christ when walking with his disciples by the way unheralded and unknown, and yet producing the most exquisite sensations of pleasurable emotion by his gracious words. He drifted away from that evening meeting as silently and unknown as he came, and yet he had left the impress of his sweet spirit and intense fervor. Next was he seen in the Sunday morning congregation, when he presented his church letter from one of the New York pastors, and thus became identified with us in church labor.

We look at this man's career and trace his short life's history in its many vicissitudes with the most intense interest, as it reveals to us such stupendous value of adhering to principle, no matter where such adherence leads or whatsoever sacrifice it involves. Precious indeed, in all ages of the church, have been the exhibitions of Christian steadfastness under the severest tests. Job's integrity, Daniel's faithfulness, and the Hebrew children's devotion shine out as the sparkle of the pure diamond, and beautifully illustrate how little does the devout heart care for the glitter of earthly emolument when offered for the sacrifice of stern Christian principle. And so did the conduct of this young man sparkle with intensest luster when the test came; for come it did with terrible severity not long after he reached this city.

In that day of California history the popular idea in all parts of the world seemed to be that if the impecunious could only reach our golden shores, they would want no more, as golden streams were constantly running down our streets in such swift and overflowing current that none need go unsupplied; and so many under this delusion left their homes with only money enough to bring them here. Upon their arrival, however, the hallucination vanished, and they found themselves in a strange land where life's necessities could not be secured without large expenditure of solid coin. It was not remarkable, under these circumstances, that much suffering was endured and much want and privation experienced. Nor was it strange that the labor market was overstocked, insomuch that men were found by thousands who could not obtain remunerative employment. Such was the state of things when this young man found his home among us, and he, having a wife to support and not much money to meet their ever recurring wants, was extremely anxious to obtain employment. Many a day did he plod the streets, weary and disheartened, in search of some mode of honestly earning the necessary means of support. Although gifted with business talent of no mean order, yet the opportunity to put that talent to useful service did not occur till his money was about gone, and his courage had well nigh failed. And then that opportunity came only in the form of most severe temptation. He was offered a fine situation where the pay was large and the work not over exhaustive; but with it was coupled the necessity of violating God's commandment in the desecration of his holy day. None could acceptably fill the situation unless he worked on the Sabbath, and without consenting to do this the situation was not at his command. What should he do—allow his wife and himself to starve or accept the tempting offer? On the one hand was comfort and plenty, on the other penury and want. On the one hand was independent self-support, while on the other was only suppliant beggary. Not much time would be required to determine the question in the case of one less grounded in moral principle, or firmly rooted in his attachment to religious duty. But this young man had dwelt too long in the secret place with the Most High; he had communed too deeply with the Master, and been too fully baptized with His Spirit to hesitate for a moment in rejecting the demoralizing proffer. He could suffer the pangs of hunger longer if need be; he could waste in flesh and pine in spirit; he could wander about these streets in quest of honest toil, till, foot-sore and weary, he might sink and die; but to disobey God, to deny the blood that bought him, to sell his convictions of right for paltry gold, or even for bread to sustain the life of her who was dearer far to him than the life that beat in his own breast, never! Proudly did he exclaim, "God forbid that I should do this thing," and so did he triumph grandly in asserting his manly adherence to duty and to God. Soon relief came, but came in a severe manner. The man of God who had the contract for building this church gave him employment in hauling brick from the wharf to the place where the temple was to be reared. And so he went down into the menial service of a day laborer, driving a mule and cart loaded with brick through these streets, rather than take a position for which he was better fitted by nature and education, in which was involved the necessity of violating his conscience by disobeying God.

Subsequently this man became the first superintendent of the Central Sabbath school, which institution still bears the marks of his wise oversight, and owes much of its present prosperity to the strong foundations for its support which he reared in the years long ago. He also was one of the first-class leaders of that church, and night and day did he labor for its success, till consumption's fang fastened upon the delicate frame of his saintly wife, and made their removal from this coast a necessity. But the removal did not avert the evil. It came on swift wing, and he laid her precious remains away to sleep in Jesus till the Resurrection morn. Shortly after her demise he gave himself to the ministry, and became a member of an Eastern Conference. His race however, was short; for excessive labor and undue exposure brought on the disease of which his wife died, and after lingering a few months he went to join her in the skies, where they two are forever with the Lord. He, no doubt, now realizes the extreme wisdom of uncompromising fidelity to Christ, in the midst of severe temptation to deviate from the strict line of religious duty.

AN IRREPRESSIBLE.

Sometime in 1858 there appeared at our altars, with church letter in hand, a candidate for reception into church fellowship. There was much about the man that was peculiar, and some things that were specially striking in his personal appearance and personal conduct. In the first place, he was greatly deformed in having no feet. These he had lost through exposure in the mountains; for they had become so badly frozen that amputation was necessary to save life. And this had been performed in the rudest manner possible, as no skillful surgeon was present, when the necessity arose, to perform the painful operation. Nor had the rude operators any delicate or refined instruments at their command with which to remove the mortifying members. Coarse saws and heavy knives were all the exorcising instruments which could be secured in those mountain fastnesses at that early day ; and so these sturdy, untutored mining surgeons used the best tools they had to relieve their suffering companion of his decayed members. Rude as were the operators, and coarse as were the instruments, still the work was done in so successful a manner as to preserve the life of the patient, and there he stood on his stumps before God's altar, pledging eternal fealty to the King of kings and Lord of lords.

But not only was this man singular in personal appearance, but he was exceedingly so in personal conduct, for he had many habits which were eccentric to the last degree. Prominent among these was the habit of vociferous shouting. Sudden as the lightning's flash, loud as the thunder's deafening roar, and startling as an electric shock from a full-charged battery, would that irrepressible shout come. When all was calm as a summer's eve, with not a zephyr of excitement to stir the sensibilities of the most susceptible, that shout would come—come it would in the most unexpected manner, and at the most unexpected time. Come to shock and horrify the quivering sensibilities of nervous women ; come to disgust and outrage the feelings of sturdy men: come to offend all sense of good taste and all rules of conventional propriety: and yet come it would, and nothing could suppress it. Church censure was inadequate: Official Board pronunciamentos were ineffectual; public pastoral reprimands had no effect: and so the thing went on at all social meetings: nay more, for even on all preaching occasions that irrepressible shout would invariably go off, to the extreme discomfort of all present.

It was not unfrequently amusing in the extreme, to witness the effect of these explosions on that part of the congregation in his immediate vicinity. Everything would be going on orderly, and the sermon apparently producing a salutary effect on the attentive and interested listeners, when, sudden as the earthquake's tread, would come that awful shout, as shrill and shrieking as the calliope's most startling scream. Then would timid ones spring from their seats in frenzied fright, as though pierced by an electric shock, and their efforts to recover their self-possession, after the spasm, would give the whole matter such an air of the extremely ludicrous as would almost convulse the congregation with laughter. Of course it needed not many such performances to put an end to all devotion, and render that special service of no effect for good. The nuisance was finally abated by sending the misguided, though no doubt really religious, man to his friends in the East, where, for all we know, he may be still shouting his way to heaven; as doubtless he regarded this lusty lung exercise as indispensable to his getting there. Or perhaps the dear man has ceased from his earthly toil, and gone into those beatitudes the contemplation of which so ravished his extremely impressible soul while sojourning among us. If so, his discordant notes have been changed into sweetest harmony, and his shrill, shrieking shout has rounded out into the richness of angelic melody. No more the nerve-rasping scream of the wild bird of this desert world, but from his spirit-voice there sounds forth the swelling symphony of heavenly music. And the Hallelujah comes as softly and as sweetly from him now as from any of the white-robed choristers in the grand orchestra of heaven. So does the putting on of immortality and the entrance into the glory land make all things new. So does it bring harmony out of discord, and freshness and beauty from hideous deformity.

LIGHT FROM DARKNESS.

In the winter of 1866 San Francisco was visited by Rev. Mr. Earl, a Baptist Evangelist, who came to this city in response to a call from the Ministerial Union. Of course he came to hold *union* meetings, and therefore, his visit was non-denominational, but was in the interest of Christianity in general, and no church or denomination in particular. His meetings were held in Platt's Hall, and were attended by large masses of all classes of the community. It is enough to say that these meetings were wonderfully successful in increasing the spirituality of the churches, and in adding many hundred new converts to their folds. But it seemed both to the pastor and Board of Howard St. church a waste of force to confine their efforts to the promotion of these meetings, inasmuch as not half the community could possibly be brought under their influence, for the want of room. Hundreds would be nightly turned away from these meetings, from the impossibility of wedging themselves into the dense mass who had already packed the Hall to suffocation. And so it was determined to hold a series of revival meetings at our own church, so that the overflow might have an opportunity to hear the Gospel call, and perhaps some would accept its tender pleading. Not many days elapsed before our altars were crowded with those who would see Jesus, and not a night passed without witnessing the conversion of souls.

One evening as the meeting was in progress, and the tide of religious power seemed to swell to a volume of irresistible power, an aged man was seen in the back part of the room to leave his seat and approach the altar. His hair was white as the driven snow, but his wardrobe bore evidence of long wear and scanty means. Tears were streaming from his sunken eyes, and running in brooklets down his furrowed cheeks. He was a perfect stranger to all present, and none knew from whence he came; but all saw at a glance how intensely earnest he was after the pearl of great price. His whole person was convulsed with intense feeling, and his whole being shook and throbbed like the leaves of the forest under the pressure of a mighty wind. Down on his knees he fell, and in the agony of an intensely felt want, he pleaded for Divine mercy, but seemed to plead in vain. Every eye in the vast congregation was upon him, and every Christian heart in the assembly beat with deepest sympathy for the suffering penitent. Prayer the most fervent, and pleadings the most imploring, arose in constant succession from many a devout heart in his behalf, but all to no purpose: for the intense gloom that pervaded his mind seemed impenetrable, and no ray of light could pierce the darkness so profound. And yet his insatiate desire drove him onward to a state of desperate, unyielding determination to find the object of his search or die in the attempt before leaving the place where he knelt: and when the meeting was formally dismissed, nothing could induce him to relinquish the struggle. He seemed seized with the conviction that if he went from that altar as he came, in his sins and in his blood, he would so remain to all eternity. This conviction was so deeply riveted upon his inmost thought that he pleaded in the most piteous tones to be allowed to remain where he was, that he might spend the livelong night in praying for Divine mercy. Such importunity the world never saw since the days of the Syrophenician woman. And it seemed another attempt on the part of Jesus to bring out another exhibition of that faith which laughs at impossibilities when all around is as dark and dense as Egyptain night.

Two things were apparent in this man's pleading. First, his *intensely felt want*, and second, his unwavering faith that the Man of Calvary could bring relief to his crushed and agonized spirit. And so he held with firm and unrelenting grasp the promises of God, and reckoned that however great the emergency or desperate the situation they could not fail. Sublime, indeed, was the conflict! Puny man; sin cursed and sin covered man; man whose whole life of many years had been given faithfully to the Evil One; man with naught to recommend him to the Divine favor but his helpless, dire necessity; and yet with sufficient power left to lay hold of the Divine promises and plead them fully and unyieldingly in the Divine presence. How could Christ, the sympathizing Christ, the pitying Christ, the Christ who laid down his life to redeem man and bless him when in just such an emergency, resist such an antagonist and turn a deaf ear to such pleadings? Impossible! and yet the conflict continued, and the long weary hours of the night wore away. A magic spell bound us to the spot as we knelt in the presence of this awfully sublime spectacle, and yet we doubted not the final result of this mighty conflict. The delay, however, was incomprehensible, for has He not said: "*Before* they call, I will answer them?" We know not, nor shall we know till the revealments of eternity dawn upon our vision, the reason of this delay. Nor can we comprehend why the tender and sympathizing Jesus allowed the deep anguish of this suffering penitent to continue so long. But perhaps it was to furnish us with another wrestling Jacob, and show us how mighty is puny man in the strength of his determination to prevail with God. For prevail he did: for just before the morning dawned the light from the Excellent Glory streamed into his darkened soul, and filled his anguished spirit with delight the most rapturous, and peace the most profound. Like a prince did he prevail, and a prince indeed did he become, as with his conversion passed away all low and groveling views of manhood, and his life from that day took on the noblest type of Christian devotion. He lives still to evince the power of redeeming grace to elevate and dignify the soul and life of man. And he is calmly waiting down by the river's edge till the angels come to bear him across the stream where the Man of Calvary, his best beloved, reigns. Meanwhile he is instant in season and out of season in laboring for the Master and doing what he can to promote His glory upon the earth, for he has fully learned by his own experience that "he that winneth souls is wise" beyond all the wisdom of this world. "Let him know that he which converted the sinner from the error of his way shall save a soul from death and shall hide a multitude of sins."

CHIPS.

BY REV. F. F. JEWELL.

WHOSE FAULT IT WAS.

At an official meeting some time in 1873, as the business was nearly at the end of the docket, a somewhat seedy and battered looking subject opened the door of the room where the Board was in session, and then half closed it again and stepped back into the hallway. Some one stepped to the door and asked him what was wanted. He was encouraged by the kind looks and tone of the self-constituted usher, and advanced to mutter in suppressed tone, "I want to be prayed for." He had assumed that all meetings were or ought to be "religious," which shows how benighted his mind was in such matters, and how long he had wandered from churches and church associations. He, however, was tolerated, and his "sin of ignorance winked at," and the pastor was informed that a candidate for the benefits of church and clergy was in waiting. He was asked to take a seat and wait but for a moment until the items of business on hand were disposed of, and then he should be encouraged in his healthful impulses of seeking the right way. After the matter in hand was completed, the stranger was asked to indicate his needs, and the special phases of his case which we could bear before the throne of grace in prayer. He seemed to hesitate, as if in doubt where to begin the catalogue of sins and wants; when he reached a point of decision, and dropping upon his knees, he began a prayer for himself. He acknowledged his aberrations and deflections, divergences and wanderings, in such language as he could command, until he reached the point of negotiation, when he said: "O, Lord, if you will take me back again into your favor, and forgive me for going away, if I ever backslide again it will be my own fault." Then we reflected: how representative, after all, was this somewhat amusing implication that the burden of responsibility was somewhere else than on the sinner's own head, for all the sins and follies of a bad life.

How frequently this unworthy conception is cherished, is seen in the apologies and explanations which are so frequently found on our lips. Listen to these apologies and explanations for a moment. This man pleads a constitutional excess of passions. He was born charged with such impetuous desires that no one could reasonably expect him to resist them. Another talks of the environments of life, and the social difficulties which hedge up his way to life eternal: while a third talks of the seductiveness of worldly things: and thus all seek to transfer the responsibility of their sinful practices to the Infinite Father who has created, surrounded, and endowed us in mercy and love. It is ever "our," as it was "his," own fault when we sin.

WEDDING INCIDENTS.

Upon returning to the parsonage one day, I found in waiting a pair whose errand was indicated by the relation the chairs they occupied had assumed to each other. The young woman, the bride elect, was first to speak: which fact may find an explanation in what afterwards appeared, in arranging the preliminaries to the important event. Among the usual questions in the catechism

in such cases made and provided, as the
language of the statute would have it, came
the inquiry whether either of the parties
had been in matrimonial bonds before. The
bride, whose age was given at twenty, with
a careless toss of the head, and a free and
easy air, replied: "You ought to know.
You married me yourself in this room less
than a year ago." I said: "Indeed! and
what has become of the *groom* on that occasion?" Her answer was: "He was no
good. I got rid of him." I said: "How, by
drowning or chloroforming?" She answered: "Oh, not so bad as that. I got a
divorce." I wonder if this was the case
spoken of by the wife of a divorce lawyer
in the city, who said she asked for the
grounds, when her husband informed her
that he had just procured a divorce for a
young "twain" of this neighborhood and
acquaintance, and her husband replied:
"There were no grounds, only they wanted
it. I forget now what the grounds stated
in the suit were; we only use what promises to be the most effectual in gaining the
point aimed at." What a commentary upon
the facility with which divorces may be obtained under the laws and in the courts of
California. And California is not singular
among the State sisterhood in this matter.

Is it not reasonable, upon other considerations than the regulation of family matters in Utah, that Congress should have and exercise the right to regulate this great question, and protect that institution that furnishes to American society the real safeguards, and supports? The facility above referred to, existing in so many States of the Union, is a standing temptation to selfish, dissolute and licentious men and women all through the land, and just to the extent the temptation is felt even, the family is endangered and the nation menaced.

AFTER MANY YEARS.

Another, with an entirely different moral, and indicative of a genuine affection, which did not fade from the heart even when the rose had faded from the cheek, occurred about the same time. A man of mature years, with threads of silver glistening among the locks that clustered around a brow somewhat bronzed and beaten by the vicissitudes which had been met in the journey of life, stood before me to arrange for the ceremony which was to place him in possession of what every sensible man at that age desires, a wife. He remarked:

"She is on the Panama steamer expected to-day, and as soon as convenient after her arrival we would like to come to the parsonage for the marriage ceremony."

He lingered a little after all necessary arrangements were made, and upon a little encouragement given, perhaps, by some slight questioning, he proceeded to tell the story: first, of an early courtship in Brooklyn, N. Y., where more than twenty-five years before, "soft eyes spake love to eyes that spake again." As has been true in the experience of others "the course of true love did not run smoothly"; and social ambition on the part of the parents of the girl interfered with the plans of the young lovers, and paternal authority forbade her encouraging his bounding hopes and cherished desires of making her his wife.

Chagrined and half maddened by the reflections thus cast upon his manhood's worth, he turned his back upon the "city of churches," and what to him was more, the home of the one he loved with all the ardor of a young and true heart, and embarked for California. Here, amidst the excitements and varying fortunes of those early days, he was tossed hither and thither, until the "glittering bait was held aloft again, and Australia invited the young adventurer to try his fortunes in that far-off land of promise." There he married, and there, after a brief married life, he laid a faithful companion in the grave, and with a sad heart turned his face again toward California. Here, after years in which no word had been received from or sent to the "girl he left behind him," he chanced to meet one whom he had known in boyhood, and from whom he learned that the object of his first love was still alive. She, too, had entered into the marriage relation, had bowed in sorrow to the stroke that left her in widowhood, and was now in the "home city," doubtless wondering, at times, if ever tidings would be borne to her of the one she had never ceased to regard as having a right to her hand.

Immediately upon learning this he wrote her, and in due time an answer came. The flame which had lain latent in each bosom kindled anew, and the rest is soon told. She came, they were wedded, and the shadows went back on the dial of Ahaz, and instead of afternoon it was morning again. May many years crown the long-delayed union of two true and loving hearts.

PASTORAL WORK.

About midnight a vigorous pull at the door-bell of the parsonage awakened us from our slumbers, and a demoralized looking specimen of the soaker class appeared at the door, urging that his Riverence hasten with him to where a woman was said to be dying. We followed as he led the way from street to street and lane to alley, until we were ushered into the damp, dismal basement hallway leading to a rear tenement of a dilapidated rookery, in the cellar or basement of which, by the light of a candle, which, because of its companionship, or the foul atmosphere in which it was caught, seemed anxious to "*go out*," we saw on a pile of rags a human form, which once, perhaps, but now no longer, might be called a woman. Bloated, haggard, frenzied, in the awful horrors of delirium tremens, she was alternately shrieking and piteously pleading for rescue from the fiery scorpion fangs of the myriad hydra-headed demons which were piercing her very soul and kindling the flames of hell in every vein and artery of her already charred and loathsome body. The three or four attendants in that vestibule of Tartarus were drunk, and could only utter unintelligible babblings as we approached. We endured the sight as long as our heart would consent to remain, and utterly powerless to render aid, turned away to thread our way back again to the open air, and to the home where quiet slumber held our household in its downy arms of rest. That was only the obverse side of the wholesale liquor dealer's palatial home; the self-complacent wealthy brewer's luxurious couch; the prosperous saloon keeper's well-furnished apartments: the other end of the line, whose opening portal is the fashionable wine glass offered amid the gayeties of so-called refined society, where youth and beauty flutter around the gilded margin of this maelstrom of death, to hurl contempt toward all those whose voices are lifted to warn them of their danger.

RECEPTION OF MEMBERS FROM THE HARRISON REVIVAL.

Perhaps no scene connected with revival work in the church at any period of its history awakened more interest and delight than the reception of the Probationers, which were gathered from the meetings conducted by Thomas Harrison into full membership in the church on Sunday, May 7, 1882, when one hundred persons stood at one time, forming a hollow square extending across the altar from down both centre aisles and across the rear of the audience room, until the ends of the columns thus formed met and united. The first name called was responded to by one who arose slowly, assisted by his cane on one side and a devoted Christian wife on the other, whose four-score years had been spent in a morally "far country," and who had just returned from his bondage in that strange land; and now with that Christian wife, who had long prayed for him, was rejoicing in heirship to an inheritance incorruptible, the title deed of which had but recently been placed in his possession. In that line were here and there to be seen the bright eyes and smooth brows of childhood, as well as those of maturer years—indeed, a large proportion of the year-dates of the present century would be found represented in the birth record of those who made up the lines of that hollow square before us. The service consisted mainly of an address by the pastor, explaining and enforcing the disciplinary forms of reception, which emphasize the nature of the church as "the household of God, the body of which Christ is the head"; also, the "ends," "duties," and "privileges" of the fellowship into which they were entering. Slowly the column moved forward from left to right, and as each passed, a certificate bearing the picture of the church and giving the date and fact of admission into full church membership was placed in the hands of each one by J. K. Jones, the S. S. Superintendent, who had given full and hearty co-operation to the revival movement from the first. All who saw it admitted that it was a scene rarely exhibited in the life history of any church organization.

AN OLD FASHIONED CONVERSION.

An incident of the revival illustrating the depth of conviction produced by the pungent utterances of this phenomenal preacher and revivalist, attended by the power of the Holy Spirit, occurred in one of the evening services. The invitation had gone forth for seekers to come to the altar, and the singing was in progress, when a pleasant looking lady of about thirty years, evincing much feeling and evidently struggling to resist her convictions of duty, arose from her seat, and came rapidly along the aisle until she reached the altar, and immediately dropped on her knees and began to pray. Her frame convulsed with emotion, and there seemed pent up within her heart a Niagara of penitence seeking for repression, when suddenly she seemed to sink into a swoon, and anxious friends standing or kneeling near her seeing it, became alarmed. She was borne into the "study," which opened near the altar, and placed in a position where the anxious friends could minister to her, and use proper means for her restoration to consciousness. One proposed one thing, and one another, while the third proposed to call a physician without delay. This last counsel seemed likely to prevail, and some one was about to do so, when an old member of the church, one whose conversion occurred in the earlier days of Methodism, and had produced memories which seemed to give her tranquility, while the others were anxiously puzzled with the phenomenon at hand, said in assuring tones: "Never mind about calling a doctor; let her alone. She will come out all right. She is in the hands of the right physician now. She will recover. Let her alone, I say." A few moments of anxious waiting and watching followed, when the lips parted, the eyes gently opened, and first in whispers was heard what afterwards broke forth in audible and even in voiceful tones: "Glory to Jesus," "He saves me," "Glory, glory." She was declared convalescent, and there was rejoicing that human practitioners had not taken her out of the hands of the only One who can do helpless sinners good.

As a reminiscence, I furnish the address made by Hon. Chas. Goodall at my fifth reception as an appointee to the Howard Street Church pastorate, held at the church parlors, October 5th, 1883.

DEAR BROTHER AND PASTOR: I have been requested by members of the church to say a word of welcome to our new pastor. They seem to have an idea that I am acquainted with you, and should introduce you to them, who are strangers. But it cannot be so, for let me assure you, my dear brother, that it was with one accord they asked the Bishop to appoint you to this charge.

And it must be said they had good reason for making such request. They had heard how well you succeeded in your charge last year.

The story goes that the church where you labored last year was mortgaged for $10,000, and that under your administration it was paid off, and that all other expenses, including your own salary (alas! too small) were also paid up, and that you came to Conference with the largest collections for the benevolent institutions of the church of any charge represented.

That the people flocked to hear your preaching like doves to the windows. That you visited the members at their homes, talked and prayed with them, encouraged them in the difficulties and disappointments in life, and pointed them to the goodly land where troubles and sickness and sorrow never come. That you tenderly took the little children in your arms and blessed them. That you joined the hands of them together whose hearts but beat as one. That you laid reverently and gently away in the tomb the remains of the loved and honored dead, and comforted the mourning ones with the blessed assurance that it was their blessed privilege to meet their departed friends, "where the wicked cease from troubling and the weary are at rest."

No wonder, then, that our people hearing of all this, unanimously asked the Bishop to appoint you to this charge. And I do assure you that I speak the sentiment of each member of our society, when I say: "Inasmuch as you did it unto the least of these my brethren, you did it unto me."

Again, in the name of the church and congregation, I welcome you, our new but well known and dearly beloved pastor of the Howard Street Methodist Church.

REV. J. D. BLAIN.

BLAIN MEMORIAL.

ADDRESS BY R. McELROY.

"Death rides on every passing breeze, and lurks in every flower"; and yet, in the midst of his untiring industry, most kindly has he dealt by the pastors of this church. During her existence of some twenty-six years, but three who have ministered at her altars have been stricken down by his ruthless hand.

The scholarly Bannister, who had no peers in the realm of science or literature on this coast—a man of grand intellect, of finest culture, of purest Christian character; a valiant soldier of Christ, abounding in every good work at all times and in all places; one who seemed never to have known guile, the very soul of honor; one whose mien was saintly, whose inmost thought was pure as the virgin snow, whose aims and ambitions in life were of the most lofty and ennobling character;

whose every wish was to glorify his Maker and benefit his fellow men; a man who seemed only ignorant of the meaning of selfishness, and was continually absorbed in the luxury of living for others; such was he who was suddenly halted in life's weary march, and his itinerant journeyings abruptly ended when his sun had scarcely reached meridian. Peacefully the broken casket sleeps on the banks of the Yuba, while the jewel, bright and sparkling, adorns the Master's crown in the land of everlasting sunlight and beauty.

Geo. S. Phillips, after much toil and successful labor, fainted by the way, and was compelled to seek health in an Eastern trip; but that precious gem never again came into his possession, and his weary head lies pillowed beneath the soil of his native state of Ohio, while his sainted spirit has entered upon its wonderful life of never-ending felicity.

And now has the busy destroyer visited our altars again; for the tidings come to our ears from the distant city of Newark, N. J., that Rev. John D. Blain has languished into life by passing through the portals of death.

In the year 1861, this society was worshipping in a small wooden building on Folsom street. The congregation was meager, and the membership but a handful. The location of the church was in the midst of extensive sand dunes, and but little population surrounded it. It was, in fact, but an outpost on the skirts of the rising city. Nobly had the little band struggled to maintain its existence during the ten years of its then history. Good and true men had filled its pulpit, but all had comparatively failed to elicit much interest in the general community, in reference to this feeble vine. To reach the church one was compelled to make a Sabbath day's journey through drifting sand and howling winds. To crowd the little temple under such forbidding circumstances was a task of no mean accomplishment. And yet the newly appointed pastor, from the Conference of that year, was adequate to the task. No sooner had he entered on his work, but he began, from house to house, to seek out the lost sheep of our Israel. And this labor was not long in manifesting itself in the crowds which came flocking from every quarter of the city to his ministry. It now required more than drifting sands, or howling winds, or isolated position, to keep the people away. Brother Blain had somehow made them feel that he was their friend and brother; that he was interested in all their joys and sorrows; that he knew the heart of a stranger, and could sympathize with all who were enduring the pangs of desolate loneliness. And the number of these in the primitive days of American California history was legion. No man knew his neighbor. Every one was in the midst of a Sahara, although surrounded by myriads of human beings; for they had come from the east and the west, from the north and the south. Every nationality was represented. Every clime under the whole heaven here revealed its peculiar type of humanity. And yet for each the pastor of the little sand-hill church had a kind word, a pleasant smile of recognition, and a hearty God speed. But a little time elapsed before every body knew Brother Blain, and every body as fondly loved him.

Nor was this admiration confined to any particular sect or any particular people. Both Jew and Gentile, both Catholic and Protestant, both saint and sinner, the godless as well as the godly, merchant princes in their purple and fine linen, and paupers in their penury and rags, alike respected and honored him. For all knew that he loved them and desired to do them good, not because of their outside surroundings or their peculiar station in life, but because they were *men*, and all belonged to one common brotherhood. No wonder, then, with this universal sentiment in his favor, that his influence became as broad and far reaching as the community itself. No wonder that every man and every woman about entering the sacred portals of wedlock wanted their nuptials celebrated by Brother Blain. No wonder that all who had the remains of a loved one to be consigned to the tomb, desired the burial services to be performed by him. No wonder that when the little wooden temple became too small to accommodate the ever-increasing throng which came to listen to words of consolation and cheer drawn from the Book of God, the people came forward and poured out their money like water to provide him a more spacious edifice.

As the result of this influence and this generosity, we stand this day within the walls of this magnificent temple, for had it not been for John D. Blain this temple had not been here. He conceived the idea of its erection, he planned all its appointments, he solicited the funds to execute its building, and many a weary hour, both of body and mind, he gave freely and cheerfully to its service. In fact, so many were those hours, and so heavy were their toils, that his nervous system received its death wound in the midst of them. Never was John D. Blain the same vigorous, robust man after his departure from this pulpit, as he was before he entered it. And although he has lingered on the shores of time, some ten or twelve years since, yet his was a shattered, painful existence, which gave him but little comfort or joy.

Work, however, did he till the last, for work was his normal nature; and his highest bliss consisted in trying to build up the Redeemer's Kingdom on the earth. But he rests now. The feverish dream of life is over with him, and among the beatitudes of the skies he has entered upon a life of ever expanding, ever increasing glory.

> "Life's labor done as sinks the clay,
> Light from its load the Spirit flies,
> While heaven and earth combine to say,
> How blest the righteous when he dies."

REV. THOMAS GUARD.

GUARD MEMORIAL.

ADDRESS BY J. M. BUFFINGTON.

Dr. Thomas Guard was born in Galway County, Ireland, on the 3rd of June, 1831. His father, Rev. William Guard, left four sons, three of whom became ministers: Wesley Guard, a prominent clergyman in county Cork, Edward Guard, of Omagh, county Tyrone, and Dr. Thomas Guard—the subject of this sketch.

Dr. Guard was educated in his native county, and entered the Irish Conference at the age of 21. Six years later he married a Miss Isabel Barrett, of Dublin, by whom he had seven children—five sons and two daughters. About four years after their marriage, his wife's health being very delicate, they left Ireland for South Africa, where they remained for nine years. Dr. Guard labored earnestly in the colonies there until 1871, when he came to this country with the intention of raising money sufficient to build a church in Africa, and then of returning.

His lectures, delivered in nearly all of our principal cities, showed such power of oratory as to attract great interest. He received calls from several churches, and finally accepted that of the Mount Vernon Church of Baltimore, Md. The congregation was then known as the "Charles Street," and Dr. Guard preached in the New Assembly Rooms of that city several months before the completion of the church. At the end of three years he came to San Francisco, and accepted the pastorate of the Howard Street M. E. Church, where he remained from Sept., 1875, to Sept., 1878, meeting with marked success and making for himself staunch friends. While in this city he met with a great bereavement in the death of his wife.

At the expiration of his term with this church he moved to Oakland. From there he was recalled to Baltimore, and on the 14th of October, 1882, while yet in the prime of life, and surrounded by loving friends, his Master called him home.

The Rev. Robert Crook, LL. D., states "that from the first he was a man of great promise, distinguished as a preacher and lecturer; that he was a great reader, possessed a very retentive memory and did not take much interest in the business affairs of the church."

His intellectual gifts were remarkable. His command of language was inexhaustible, and his memory, apparently, never failed him. His articulation was rapid and rather indistinct: this, with his foreign accent, made it difficult for those unaccustomed to him to catch his words, but when once attention was attracted, his audiences were invariably impressed by his remarkable flow of words, the brilliancy of his ideas, and his own enthusiasm in his subject. He was a brilliant conversationalist, although sometimes abrupt.

"Mr. Guard's spirit was one of the most childlike simplicity; he was without tact, and could never understand our ways of doing things. If he desired to awaken the most uneducated sinner, he would appeal to him by considerations drawn from every field of thought, and expressed in language of elaborate finish and beauty. He was not a pastor. Though tender and sympathetic as a sister, systematic calls he knew not how to make, and records were an inscrutable mystery to him.

Like many other men, his defects were the excess of his qualities. He was ever and under all circumstances, first, middle, and last, an orator. With a practical man for a colleague, every one would have said: 'With Thomas Guard to preach, and his colleague to attend to everything else, the church is thoroughly furnished unto every good word and work.'"

His death came as a sudden blow to his friends. Though for four years he at times suffered great pain, he worked with much energy until the end. His last lecture was delivered a little more than a week before his death, which was caused by acute gastritis, attacks of which he had been subject to for many years.

The funeral took place from Mount Vernon Church, which was appropriately draped for the occasion. Among those present were a delegation of Methodist ministers from Philadelphia, and a number of ministers from other denominations.

At the memorial service held in the Howard Street M. E. Church, October 22, the following address was delivered by Rev. Dr. Wythe, a warm personal friend of Dr. Guard, which gives an excellent description of his character.

Dr. Wythe said:

"The duty assigned to me is not only sad but difficult, since the subject on which I am desired to address you is one of such magnitude, and so many-sided, as to require ability more than I possess. A week ago the telegraph flashed the news across the continent, that the Rev. Thomas Guard, the eloquent preacher, was dead. Few heard the tidings without a shock; they were so unexpected and unheralded. This sad event has brought us together for memorial services—a token of our respect for exalted ability and great usefulness. I have been requested to speak of the character and life of our deceased friend. It is not easy to do this, for Dr. Guard was an extraordinary man. He was like a gem covered with sparkling facets. His genius and oratory were of more than usual brilliancy. It would require his own descriptive powers, with a keener insight into character, to do him justice. Yet, as our relations were intimate, it is deemed fitting that I should speak, however imperfectly, upon this theme. I bring only a simple tribute of sincere appreciation of one who honored me as a friend, and always recognized me as a fellow-minister of the gospel of Christ. The tender sympathy in my own recent affliction is brought into strong relief by his death, and makes his removal a personal loss. 'The memory of the just is blessed,' for it proves the superiority of spiritual reality to all material good. I desire to consider our brother as a man, as a Christian, and as a Christian minister.

I. As a man: The most striking trait was a certain warmth and buoyancy of disposition which rendered him companionable. There was no assumption of dignity and superiority, nor sourness or asceticism in his manner. The Celtic fire of his heart shone from his eyes, and won to him friends from all classes of society. He seemed to live in continued sunshine, and as if he enjoyed the sunshine too. There appeared about him nothing of constraint, nothing assumed. The words and actions were natural and spontaneous; the outgushing of a nature in harmony with God's universe. His simplicity and frankness were obvious to all who knew him. He united the heart of a child with the mind of a man. Although guileless and unsuspicious of wrong designs, he was utterly incapable of policy and deceit. He could not favor, and would not stoop, either to gain the favor of the rich, or to escape from the strife of tongues. This characteristic was sometimes shown by its reaction. His contempt of duplicity in others was the very perfection of scorn. He had such a quick recognition of moral rectitude, and such a spirit of repudiation for what he deemed wrong, that he would not treat as a friend one who appeared morally unworthy. He was far more antagonistic to spiritual sins, like envy, and malice, and guile, than to others; for if sensual sins make a man a brute, spiritual wickedness renders him a fiend. What failings were seen by the eye of friendship in our brother's life seemed to spring from his artless simplicity and guilelessness, and his antipathy to anything of an opposite character.

Although lacking the drill of early and profound scholarship, he found a compensation in being an industrious and omnivarous reader of books. He had a remarkably quick perception, a most retentive memory, a poetic sensibility, and artistic power of comparison. These qualities combined to form the special bent or genius of his mind. These characteristics form the stuff of which orators are made. Had the energies

which led him to soar above the common
sphere of thought been harnessed and confined by sterner scholastic discipline, he
would have shone as a beautiful planet,
with clear, steady light. There might have
been less brilliancy, less scintillation, but
perhaps a wider orbit and a longer life.
As a man, he had interest in every human-
itarian enterprise. No good cause appealed
to him in vain. No narrow groove of
thought or creed confined his sympathies.
Whatever touched the heart or liberties of
mankind found a corresponding vibration
in his nature. As he had traveled exten-
sively, he had opportunity of studying the
condition of many people, and the forms of
government best adapted to the conform-
ation of liberty and law, and the free choice
of his mind was on the side of American
institutions. By nature and by choice he
loved the principles of American representative government.

He was as sensitive as a woman, as
patriotic as a veteran, as loving as a child,
and as impetuous as a torrent. Such men
are rare. Only a few such are met with in
a century. Such will always be attractive.
They may have enemies, for all patriotic
men—all who are worth anything—will

meet with opposition; but they will have also troops of friends, and friends who will be as true as steel. The grandeur of such characters rises above the forces of all adverse circumstances.

"As some tall cliff that lifts its awful form,
Swells from the vale, and midway leaves the storm,
Though round its breast the rolling clouds are spread,
Eternal sunshine settles on its head."

II. As a Christian, our brother was well established in the truths of evangelical religion. His faith was no blind adhesion to a mere intellectual creed, but heartfelt trust, with a clear vision of the object trusted. His reason was fully satisfied with the intellectual revelation of truth made in the Bible, and he was a student of the Scriptures above all other books. This study brought him to the spiritual revelation of the truth as it is in Jesus. A spiritual recognition of personal sin, an appropriation of the redemption made by Christ for the forgiveness of sin, a personal knowledge of actual salvation, and a constant dependence upon the sanctifying power of the Holy Spirit made our brother a real Christian. Yet he did not ignore the book of Nature, also written with the finger of God, but delighted to trace the accordance of its teaching with that of the Bible.

His piety was sincere, experimental, ardent. Though unobtrusive and not boastful, yet there was a manly vigor in his religious experience which made him ready at all suitable times to acknowledge Christ as a personal Saviour. His public prayers showed to the Christian consciousness of the church that he was a man who held communion with God. Some of his friends even preferred his prayers to his sermons. They were sometimes wonderful for unction and touching simplicity. A Presbyterian minister told me he should never forget the influence of one of his prayers, in which he referred to all the mercies of our Father as tender mercies, and to all his kindnesses as loving kindness. No man could pray as he prayed who did not live near the heart of God.

III. As a minister, he regarded the pulpit as his sphere. His personal characteristics rendered it peculiarly appropriate to him. Whatever he may have been outside the pulpit, there he was an ambassador from God, a herald of the sovereign King. The splendor of his oratory and the wealth of his mind were made there garlands for the cross of Christ. He wielded the sword of the Spirit with such incisive discrimination that it often became a discerner of the thoughts and intents of the heart. The love manifest on Calvary, and the supreme glory of Christ were themes which fired his soul with almost seraphic ecstasy.

His sermons showed careful preparation and a most remarkable memory. Many of his most brilliant passages were very carefully studied; yet inspired with his theme, he sometimes soared far beyond all previous thought. The style was antithetical and ornate, but he often required an elaborate introduction to bring him into sympathy with his subject, so that his mind could have full play. To some persons this was tedious, especially to those who love to recline at their ease in church, and have the Gospel diluted and strained in fifteen-minute sermonettes; but to the thoughtful and refined, the sermons of our brother were an intellectual and a spiritual feast, and the church was generally crowded with such hearers.

His public lectures, as well as his sermons, grappled with the religious questions of the age and left a marked impression. Few that heard will soon forget the scene in his lecture on the influence of the Bible on the age, which represented a skeptic trying to obliterate the marks of the Bible on civilization; ransacking the public and private libraries to erase Christian thought from literature; going to our court-houses and halls of record to eliminate A. D. from all our title-deeds; and to our state-houses to remove all traces from legal and constitutional enactments; and even stooping down in our cemeteries, chisel in hand, to chip all Christian references from the grave-stones of our honored dead. The public tested his oratorical powers perhaps too severely for his strength, but they were not found wanting in the cause of truth and religion. No college of learning honored itself by conferring upon him the Doctorate, which in a by-gone age was the synonym for teacher; but the great college of the public recognized his worth and teaching qualities; and to the public he is known, and will be, as Dr. Guard. He had a generous catholic spirit, and a true Christian fellowship with other denominations; yet he was conscientiously attached to the doctrines and usages of Methodism, and regretted to see in his own church any variation from what he deemed the true spirit of the denomination. He especially condemned the laying aside of the grand and beautiful poetry of Charles Wesley for the ryhming jingle of our modern social songs. He regarded it as an offense to good taste, spiritually. The *esprit de corps* of the Methodist ministry was to him delightful, and this was one of the chief attractions of Baltimore, where he had seen it in such perfection. How often he expressed a wish that it might flourish here as there, and how often he had fostered the sentiment by preaching and lecturing for churches in the country who were too poor to pay their preacher's salary!

His death is a loss to this coast as well as to the church at large. The memory of such ministers is precious. The church cannot afford to pass them by. The homage paid by such minds to the cross of Christ is an argument for the truth and divinity of Christianity. Here, at least, in this new country, so full of materialism and materialistic tendencies, the memory of our brother's oratory, so spiritual and so biblical, is a precious legacy to the church which will not soon be forgotten. Our brother is now at rest. With other ministers of our church, who have labored here for the Master and have been called home, he has entered upon his reward. "They rest from their labors, and their works do follow them."

"'And so he giveth his beloved sleep,'
   As seemeth to him best ; O ! blessed thought
God's holy Writ hath through the ages brought
To comfort those that sorrowful must weep,
Nor leave them desolate ; our cross of woe
Is by the priceless words of Christ made light ;
His consolation, sorrow's darkest night
So sweet illuminates, that we may go
Rejoicingly, that 'death hath lost its sting,
The grave, its victory' ; the friends we love
Will in God's golden harvest fields above
In his good time know perfect blossoming ;
And all these heavy griefs that make life dim
But draw the suffering children closer him."

REV. J. T. PECK, D. D.

PECK MEMORIAL.

ADDRESS BY REV. F. F. JEWELL.

Jesse Truesdell Peck was born in Middlefield, Otsego County, N. Y., Aug. 14, 1811, and died in Syracuse, N. Y., May 18, 1883. He was one of eleven children—five sons and six daughters—all of whom became members of the Methodist Episcopal Church; the five sons entering the ministry of the church in which the parents lived and died.

When I was pastor of the church in Oswego, N. Y., from which I was transferred to this in 1872, I had as my assistant a venerable father in the ministry, Rev. Reuben Reynolds, who was for some time district school teacher in the neighborhood where the family of Luther Peck, father of Jesse, resided. In Dr. George Peck's autobiography, I find this allusion to my friend: "My teacher was Reuben Reynolds, then, like myself, a licensed exhorter in the church, now an honored member of the

Northern N. Y. Conference. This was in 1815–16, which would find Jesse a child of four or five years. From Father Reynolds I learned very many things concerning the remarkable home that graduated so many sons into the ministry, and of the child Jesse, of whom my friend always delighted to say with his characteristic quaintness: "I taught him his letters, and I am glad I did; he has made such good use of them."

He was licensed as a local preacher at the early age of eighteen. Three years afterward, when twenty-one years old, he joined the old Oneida Conference, and commenced his itinerant career, with no other idea in his heart than to give all his years to this work, for which he seemed so well fitted, even from the beginning. His consecration, however, implied obedience to the voice of the church, and there was no hesitation when he was taken by that voice, and for sixteen years required to bear the usual, and in some cases, the unusual burdens, borne by the early educators in our Methodism. Five years afterward he was chosen Principal of Gouverneur Wesleyan Seminary, St. Lawrence County, N. Y. Here I found his name fragrant in many families and circles, where, long years afterwards, I was permitted to enter. Here in his home his parents lived, and here his mother died.

Of this mother it was written at that time: she was a true mother in Israel, kind and conciliatory in disposition, firm and patient under trials, praying without ceasing with strong and victorious faith, fervent in spirit serving the Lord. She had a sympathetic heart, which prompted her to care for the sick and the poor, and seek diligently the wandering, the discouraged, and the reckless. Her burning zeal impressed all who came into her presence. The giddy and the profane were struck dumb by her tender reproofs uttered in well-chosen words and in the spirit of kindness, and her desire for the salvation of souls often engaged her in personal efforts which won them to the Savior. She early consecrated her children to God, and sought by precept and example to lead them to Christ. They were all converted. Two of her daughters died before her in holy triumph, and she lived to see all her sons in the Gospel ministry. When she heard the last one of them preach, she said: "Now Lord, lettest thou thy handmaiden depart in peace, for mine eyes have seen thy salvation." Of her death, Rev. Dr. Wentworth, then her pastor, said it was peaceful and triumphant— a fitting close to such a life. The venerable servant of God (alluding to her husband) was waiting to close the eyes of the companion of his youth. The breeze of an autumnal evening rustled the drapery of a open window, but besides this there was no sound, save the deep breathing of the aged sufferer. Suddenly the soft, silvery, tremulous voice of the white-haired veteran fell upon the ear: " Give joy or grief; give ease or pain; take life or friends away, etc."

" I fancied," says the Dr., " that the dying saint listened to the music of two worlds, and listening, smiled and died." I have inserted this glimpse of his mother, that in the analysis of the character of our departed friend, due credit may be given to the one who under God gave directions to, and to indicate from whom he inherited, some of the most striking traits of his beautiful character. His pulpit power was here recognized, and his services sought on various occasions, as an able and talented preacher of the word.

This power was felt, however, to most advantage in the school, where in remarkable revivals, his emotional oratory was made a means of awakening many a young man, who afterwards entered the ranks of the Christian ministry. Here occurred what was perhaps representative of the times, as an incident in revival work.

Governeur was, and has generally been, a strong Presbyterian community. The Presbyterian minister sometimes attended the chapel services, and was careful, especially when revival meetings were in progress, to lend his presence in the interest of religious decorum and propriety. On one of these occasions the altar was crowded with penitents, and there were sobs mingled with earnest prayers from stricken penitents on every side. The Presbyterian minister, in looking about, saw among those weeping ones a child of his own flock sobbing as violently as any. He approached her, and taking her by the arm raised her to her feet, and leading her to one of his Elders who was just at hand, he said: "Take this girl out of doors: she needs fresh air." The Principal firmly said: "She needs salvation." "Let us pray for her."

From Governeur he was transferred to the Troy Conference, and placed in charge of the Troy Conference Seminary at West Poultney, Vt., in the spring of 1841. A wider field here opened before the already successful young Principal. The academy building was large and beautiful, costing $40,000 at a period when building was far less expensive than now.

Here, with a corps of professors under him, most of whom became eminent in after years in the field of instruction and literature, he commanded the respect and confidence of all for his geniality, energy, and wisdom in administration. Here, as at Gouverneur, extensive revivals prevailed in the Seminary. Dr. Stephen D. Brown, of precious memory in the Troy Conference, was wont to speak of a sermon preached at one of the revival meetings in the school by the young Principal, as the most powerful sermon to which in a lifetime he ever listened.

From this he was elected President of Dickinson College, at Carlisle, Pennsylvania, where he remained four years. He then served a term as pastor of Foundry Church, Washington, D. C., at the close of which he was elected general secretary and editor of the Tract Society of the Methodist Episcopal Church. One term in the pastorate of the Green Street Church, N. Y., completed his labor in the East, previous to his transfer to this Conference and his labors on this coast. Of these another will speak. After his return to the East he served three charges, viz.: Peeksville, Hudson Street, Albany, and Centenary, Syracuse, where he was when elected to the Episcopacy in 1872. He was one of the founders, and I may say, the chief founder of the Syracuse University; president of the first board of trustees, and to it he gave untiring labor, and all of his considerable fortune.

I well remember his ringing words in the State Convention of which he was chairman; which convention gave indorsement and form to the great ideas which had filled the great mind of this truly great man.

He was five times a member of the General Conference, and a fraternal delegate to the Canadian and East British Conferences. As an author he has given to his church and ages several valuable and some standard works, viz.: "The Central Idea of Christianity," "The True Woman—or Life and Happiness at Home and Abroad," "What Must I Do to be Saved," and "The History of the Great Republic from a Christian Standpoint."

It was while he was engaged in this work

I first met him, and an acquaintance began which has been a pleasure and a benediction to me ever since. I was invited to his home. He was very busy in his literary labors. I spoke of the research and labor involved in his work. He replied, with a beaming face: "But, oh, it pays to trace the footprints and handiwork of our Heavenly Father along the line of the ages." His transfer soon afterward to the Conference of which I was a member, brought me into frequent contact with him after that, and served to produce what I felt honored to claim, a growing friendship between us. I have been associated with him at several dedications. I have heard him preach as but few men, living or dead, ever could preach, on great occasions, when the gospel would roll from his lips an avalanche of convincing and saving power. I sat beside him in the delegation as a member of the General Conference which elevated him to the Episcopacy. He was the first one to intimate to me that I was to be sent to San Francisco, and placed in charge of Howard Street Church. In that letter he said: "My Dear Jewell, if the way opens, as it seems to be doing, and duty says so, I know you will go."

He kindly wrote me a long letter on the eve of my departure for your midst, and gave me such counsel as was prompted by his great fatherly heart, and I flattered myself to believe a special interest in me as a a friend. Among other things he said: "Trust the official members of the Howard Street Church; I know them." He has kindly written me from time to time, although his work has been so absorbing, his last note being one of congratulation upon the improvement made last year in our church property. I mention these to express my feelings to-day. Bishop Peck was my personal friend, and whoever had his friendship had the friendship of as true a heart as ever throbbed in a human bosom. Of his last sickness we have learned but little beyond this; that while otherwise enfeebled by sickness, pneumonia attacked him, and by it he was so prostrated as to be able to speak only in whispers, and was unconscious most of the time. His record was on high; and he has passed on to his treasure and the society of the redeemed in heaven. His life and labors are the legacy of the church —let us use it wisely.

ADDRESS BY R. McELROY.

Death, the mighty reaper, is still busy; oh, how busy! Not a moment's rest, and never weary. His gleaming sickle, with keenest edge, is ceaselessly leveling the tender shoot as well as the ripened grain. All ages, all classes, are stricken by his sturdy blows, and garnered for the mighty harvest. None are exempt; the good and the pure, as well as the evil and the vicious —all fall in their time, and are hidden from mortal view. Why, then, should this pulpit escape the general fiat? Why should heaven be unpeopled from this sacred desk? Why should that shining shore have no representative from this platform? If they come from the East and the West, from the North and the South, to sit down with Abraham in the kingdom of heaven, why should not God allow some who have stood here pointing pilgrims up to those golden thrones, to nestle very tenderly within the bosom of the glorified patriarch? Surely, our work in this temple would be fruitless indeed, if the priests who minister at its altars are not permitted to go, when they weary in life's battle, to that favored seat where the harpers harp, and the redeemed sing.

We come then, on this memorial day, not to sadden our hearts with mournful dirges that our loved and revered are gone, but to gladden our spirits that they are counted worthy of so great honor as being released from earthly labor and crowned with immortal glory. We rejoice that to-day, among those who stand upon the sea of glass mingled with fire, are those who once stood where we now stand, and told us of the blood which made them pure. Lips that clearly and forcefully announced the wondrous plan of salvation from this altar are now attuned to celestial melodies, and sing, oh, how sweetly, " the song of Moses and the Lamb!" No cause, then, have we for sighs and tears, no room for bitter lamentation that Heath and Phillips, that Bannister and Blain, that Guard and Peck have left the damps of earth for the brightness and beauty of heaven.

My acquaintance with Jesse T. Peck began in the year 1846. He was then the honored and successful Principal of Troy Conference Academy, in Poultney, Vermont. The next year I entered the ministry of the same Conference, and from that hour we have held the most precious intimacies, personal when together, through corres-

pondence when separated. After leaving
the Troy Conference Academy he went to
Carlisle, Penn., and assumed the Presidency
of Dickinson College. From that institution he became General Secretary of the
Tract Society of the M. E. Church. Upon
retiring from this position he went back
into the pastorate, and was appointed to the
Green Street charge, New York City.
After the expiration of the constitutional
term at Green Street, he was transferred to
the California Conference, and appointed
pastor of Powell Street church in this
city. This was in the year 1858. As soon
as he entered upon his pastorate he became
most closely identified with the cause of
Methodistic Christianity on this coast.
There was no department of the general work
that did not claim his sympathy and share
his toil. Specially among these were the
California Christian Advocate and University of the Pacific. The columns of the
former were constantly, during all his sojourn on this coast, enriched and embellished
with stirring articles from his *facile* pen ;
while the prosperity of the latter was
greatly enhanced by his wise counsels in
the Board of Trustees, and his liberal contributions to its needy exchequer. He was

at once regarded by other denominations as a prince in our Israel, and as such was accorded a prominent place in all non-denominational Christian enterprises. While intensely loyal to his own church, he was nevertheless entirely divested from sectarian bigotry, and hence was a general favorite with all catholic-spirited, Christ-loving men. None loved him more, nor regretted his departure from the coast to a greater extent, than did men outside of Methodism, who had learned to esteem his worth by association in all causes conducive to human weal. These men made him President of the California Bible Society, an office which he retained while he remained on the coast, and which he, at all times, most fully magnified. At the time of his election that Society was in a very straightened condition financially, and what little property it had was grievously burdened with debt. But through his wise counsels, far-reaching plans were inaugurated, which matured into very great advantage to the Society, freeing it entirely from debt, and giving it large material interests and great spiritual usefulness. And so everything he touched, whether Methodistic or non-denominational, seemed to feel the life-giving current of his magic wand.

After serving the Church at Powell Street, Sacramento, Santa Clara, and in the San Francisco District, he came to us and assumed the pastorate of this church. Such was the condition of the charge at that time that no ordinary man could have had the least possible chance of success. We had just reared and dedicated this temple, and were loaded down with a debt of $14,000, after every member and friend of the society had given his last possible dollar to the enterprise and every legitimate available outside means to raise funds had been exhausted. One of the most indefatigable and efficient pastors that Methodism had ever known, the Rev. John D. Blain, had just vacated the charge, and been appointed to inaugurate a new enterprise but a few blocks to the westward. Of course, the whole people loved Bro. Blain, and greatly desired to aid him in his new field. To give him a start and form a nucleus upon which he could lean, a colony of some forty of our most earnest Christian workers went out from us. Of course, in our debt-burdened condition, this loss was quite a severe strain on the society. And not only so, but many, very many non-members who formed a part of this congregation were so in love with Bro. Blain, and so respected him for his untiring and unselfish labors in their behalf, that they, too, went out from us to become part of the new congregation. Under these circumstances, had not the new pastor been a man of extraordinary power, both as pastor and preacher; had he not been vested with wonderful magnetic force to attract the people; had he not been replete in wise and feasible schemes to advance the cause committed to his charge, the Society would have languished under his ministry, and failure would have been written over the door of his administration. But to the contrary, so great was his pulpit eloquence, so massive and beautiful his thoughts, so fervid and burning his zeal, so heart-thrilling his exhortations, so soul-inspiring his prayers, so steady and pure his piety, so sweet and guileless his spirit, so tender and helpful his sympathy, so unceasing his pastoral labors, so affable and gentlemanly his deportment, so genial and sunny his intercourse with all, that but little time was required to fill the seats which had been vacated, and make his pastorate an assured success. Indeed, so great was that success and so opulent were his resources that he had all times, and on all occasions, ample means to further assist and foster the infant Central. No two men ever loved each other more or worked in more perfect harmony than did Jesse T. Peck and J. D. Blain. No jealousy or strife ever existed between them, no anxiety as to which should be the greatest in the kingdom of the people's esteem. But with one heart and with one mind each endeavored to the very utmost of his ability to build up the common cause.

As Dr. Peck had been at the head of several of our educational institutions before coming to this coast, and had spent many years in educating young men for the various learned professions, he conceived the idea of organizing the young men of his church into a literary society, that they, by church associations, might improve their intellectual status as well as their spiritual condition. Accordingly, an unemployed evening was designated for their meeting, and a room in the basement of the church assigned them. Not many weeks elapsed before the society grew to large proportions and became quite a feature of our church work, and very many young men of a literary turn were brought under church influences through its instrumentality. There is no doubt the society was exceedingly useful, in a high sense, to most of its members. Not only did the pastor have care over the flock in all their spiritual interest, not only did he look sharply after the prayer and class meetings, the Sunday school and Bible classes, but every department of church work was constantly upon his hands and his heart. Busy, oh! how busy was his life in Howard Street! And then that debt, that ponderous debt, was a matter of great solicitude to him; so much so that he set on foot a plan to reduce it during his first year. Ten thousand dollars of this debt was funded in a mortgage upon the property, and four thousand dollars was carried on the trustees' notes as floating. The plan was to pay off and cancel this floating portion of the liability, and a subscription was opened on condition that all must be raised or none would be payable. That subscription had reached only the sum of $3,200, and all the material had been fully worked up when the Board met for counsel. We canvassed the subscription, we canvassed the church record, and not a member of the Board could see where another dollar could be got. Sad, sullen

and despairing we sat thinking that the
$3,200 would be sacrificed for the lack of
the $800, and were about to adjourn in
utter despair, when the pastor stealthily
drew from his pocket a bit of paper, and
passed it over to me as Treasurer of the
Board. Judge of the electrical effect upon
that body of anxious men, when I announced
to them that the bit of paper was a certi-
fied check for $800, which the pastor had
picked up among his Front-street merchant
friends during the day, just to meet this
contingency, and round out the full sum of
the floating debt. No member of the
church knew what he was doing that day,
but the sequel showed that he had been
gleaning well. It also showed how large
and potent was his influence over the men
of the mart, who only gave from personal
respect for him, and not from any special
attachment to the church.

It must not be inferred, however, that he
was entirely beyond the shafts of envy.
No man with positive opinions, with pre-
eminent success in his life-work, can ever
reach that goal until he enters the Golden
City. Such is the extreme selfishness of
humanity, that many are found who try to
exalt themselves by hurling venomous shafts

at those whose lofty positions they fain would reach. I have seen such shafts enter his extremely sensitive nature, and have witnessed how terrible were their effects in lacerating his finest and most delicate feelings; but never on this green earth of ours have I witnessed so much Christlike forbearance, such an indisposition on being reviled to revile again, such an entire absence of all vindictiveness toward those whose calumnies have made the heart quiver with intensest anguish. In all my closest intercourse with this noble man, I cannot recall a single unkind word uttered by him in regard to any human being.

His devotion to his sick wife took him from this coast, and kept him a resident of the East, as the climate there was better adapted to her enfeebled condition. And so this family affliction robbed us of his valuable services, and lost to us all that he might have achieved for the cause, had he been permitted to stay and labor. But our loss was the gain of others, for surely he has not been idle. With hand and heart, and brain and tongue, and pen and purse all consecrated to the one great cause that charmed his boyhood life; that held spellbound his manhood days; that lost none of

its magic sweetness when the infirmity and
decrepitude of age came on; that upheld
and sustained him when death's cold waters engulfed him. Idle? No! nor is he
idle now. Dead though he is, yet speaking still; and will forever speak along the
ages yet to come. From leaf and page,
from book and tract, from memory's deep
recess, speaking firm and strong, speaking
sweet and silvery, speaking words of cheer
to weary pilgrims, speaking words of
warning to wayward ones. Hark! don't
you hear the echo of his wondrously sonorous voice, as it comes along through all the
corridors of years agone, when from this
sacred desk it trembled upon the air, and
filled all this sacred temple with richest
melody? Dead? Yes, but still alive forever more! Alive to enjoy the fruitions
of the heavenly land! Alive to be free
from the pains and agonies of earth!
Alive to look up, up, up at the wondrous
glories of that land where no night is;
where the sun goes not down, and where
the springtime of youth and beauty is forever more; where flowers do not fade and
grasses are ever green; where beauty vies
with beauty, and where splendor rolls on
splendor; where the jasper walls are seen

and the Eden groves flourish. Yes, alive to shine as the brightness of the firmament, and as the stars, forever. Alive to behold the King in his beauty, and witness his wonderful coronation by the armies of heaven. Alive to go on from glory to glory as eternal ages roll. Alive to take in the swelling symphonies of angelic choirs, and feel the ravishing joy which those symphonies impart. Alive to witness the unfolding of what had been mysterious providences in life's history, and to see how fully those seemingly hard providences had conduced to the highest good. So is he alive to-day, and so will he ever be alive as eternal cycles move. Forever with the Lord, Amen—so let it be.

ADDRESS BY REV. DR. WYTHE.

Among the apostolic men connected with the early history of the Christian Church, we find representatives of every class of Christian ministers. Barnabas appears most nearly to typify the chief characteristics of Bishop Peck. This surname of Barnabas, signifying son of exhortation or consolation, was given by the apostles to Joseph, a Levite of Cyprus. We first read of him as being at Jerusalem about the time of the Ascension, and selling his land to bring the price of it into the common fund of the church. After this he was sent to Antioch to encourage the disciples, and it is said of him that he was a good man and full of the Holy Ghost and of faith. His succeeding history is connected with the missionary labors of St. Paul. His commanding appearance led the people at Lystra, who supposed that the gods had come down to them in the likeness of men, to call him Jupiter, while Paul, who was the chief speaker, was termed Mercurius.

His personal appearance, his liberality, his comforting exhortations, his personal faith, the pureness of his life, and the evident unction of the Holy Ghost, suggest to us the characteristics of the friend and Bishop whose loss we mourn to-day.

I have been desired to give some personal reminiscences of Bishop Peck, with a brief analysis of his character; but I realize that whatever I may say will fall far short of being a portrait, but will only be an imperfect sketch. The remembrance of goodness in our friends should stimulate our efforts for personal excellence, and since our departed friend was a bright example of unselfish devotion, even an imperfect review of his character will be useful.

My first acquaintance with Bishop Peck was in January, 1863—a little over twenty years ago. I had heard him preach before that, and had once casually met him when acting as visiting committee at Dickinson College, Carlisle. It was about the darkest period of the war of the rebellion, and accumulated disasters had discouraged many. Greenbacks were down to forty cents on the dollar. I had been transferred from the medical charge at Camp Parole, Alexandria, to the Department of the Pacific, and had narrowly escaped capture by the Alabama. The government owed me four months' back salary and transportation, and I had to pay my own passage-money and that of my family, in addition to the sacrifice of my business, library, and household goods at a forced sale. I had been appointed surgeon at Camp Union, Sacramento, and attached to the staff of General Wright; but I had become reduced to the last twenty dollars when I arrived with my family at the hotel. My Presiding Elder and the Preachers' Meeting at Philadelphia had given me letters of recommendation to the ministers of this coast, and with these I started to find Dr. Peck, who was the pastor of the Sixth street Church. A heartier and more brotherly greeting I never received. I told him frankly my circumstances, and he gave me judicious advice. Not content with this, he aided me to find a suitable home for my family, went with me and became security for the payment of my household goods, and in all possible ways showed the kindness of a brother in my need. His conduct in this instance indicated the real nature of the man.

He was intensely patriotic. His voice and influence sustained the government all through the war. He was profoundly impressed with the conviction that the cause of the Nation was a righteous one, and that God would lead it to a successful issue. In my own case he saw the claim, not only of friendship, but of patriotism. Had opportunity served, he would have sacrificed position and property, and even life if necessary, for the nation. As it was, he used position and property for the nation's cause. Few men in California did more to uphold the government, even when the case seemed desperate.

He was full of brotherly kindness. No

one made his acquaintance without realizing that. His was no narrow, niggardly spirit, looking out for opportunities for self-aggrandizement. His sympathies went out in a full stream, and attracted to him people of all classes of society. No man was better known nor more esteemed here, during the eight years he spent upon this coast, than Dr. Peck.

He was generous even to those who opposed him. No man can escape antagonisms, and the more noble the spirit, or more conspicuous the person, the greater will be the liability to captious criticism and persecution from the envious or the malicious. Dr. Peck did not escape from such attacks, but he never allowed them to disturb his equanimity. He made allowance for the weaknesss and temptations of human nature, and never suffered a spirit of retaliation to irritate his breast. Like the man in white, described by Bunyan, against whom the black man was constantly throwing mud, the mud rolled to his feet and the raiment remained white as before.

He was a truly Christian man. He was not merely attached to Christ, but he had experienced the renewing power of Christ. The unction of the Holy One was a reality in his soul. His life was one of prayer and communion with spiritual things. All he had was consecrated to God, and he enjoyed a constant assurance that his consecration was accepted. During several years of close intimacy with him I found his religious spirit and experience a personal benediction, and I have heard many testify to the same thing.

As a Christian minister he might be surpassed in learning and natural eloquence, but few equalled him in that fervid eloquence which results from the inspiring presence of the Holy Spirit, and none excelled him in fidelity. While associated with him as a fellow-laborer in San Francisco, I was often led to admire his earnest, persistent zeal, and indefatigable efforts to promote the work of Christ.

He was naturally a leader among men. His executive ability was of a very high order. This was recognized at Sacramento, when, during a dead-lock, as it was called, in the legislature, the political leaders were willing to compromise by offering him the United States Senatorship. He came to me that evening for my opinion, and I advised him to pray over it, and act as conscience dictated. The next morning he told me that he had decided to decline the flattering offer, as it would divorce him from the ministry. I confess that he then appeared to me sublime. Such a sacrifice of personal ambition could only have proceeded from the heroism of faith.

I remember, also, a time when his capacity for administration was severely tested. It was at the General Conference of 1872, shortly after his election as bishop. The members of that Conference were very numerous, as it was the first time that laity and ministers had been associated in the supreme council of our church. The hall was large, and speakers sometimes so irrepressible that it was difficult to preserve parliamentary order. Bishop Peck was to preside for the first time, and, as he had been the unanimous choice of the Pacific Coast delegation, it was natural that some solicitude should be felt concerning his success. Able men and important questions had to be held firmly in the hands of the president. But our bishop proved himself to be the peer of the rest, and congratulations were heartily exchanged. After this, there was no doubt of his ability to govern.

He was tender and simple as a child. All great minds have child-like simplicity, which renders them incapable of guile. Dr. Peck rose to high position among his brethren by no dubious, crooked or slimy ways, but by pursuing the even tenor of his life with a frank and hearty sincerity. His simplicity of soul could not be comprehended by those who cultivate the art of concealment and political intrigue. The difference between them is as that between the owl and the eagle—one delighting in the pure sunlight and open sky, and the other seeking the dark recess in the night.

He had a cosmopolitan and liberal spirit. His sympathies were not confined to Methodism; and he was loved and honored in other denominations for his Christian courtesies as well as his abilities. Yet he loved the Methodist doctrine and polity as the best exponent of Christian faith, and the best evangelizing system in the world.

His method of contributing to religious education is a model for those who have but a moderate income. A few men only become rich, and if we depend wholly upon these for the endowment of our needy colleges and other necessary evangelizing agencies, it will be imperfectly done, to say nothing of the slavery to rich men which necessarily follows such dependence. Dr.

Peck was not a rich man, but he sagaciously planned to make the most out of his opportunities. He and his beloved wife agreed to carry a joint life insurance policy in favor of Syracuse University, which, at the Bishop's death, obtains a considerable sum. Other benevolences were of frequent occurrence during his life. Our own University of the Pacific was not forgotten, and personal acts of generosity can be recalled by others besides myself.

He died May 18th, at his home in Syracuse, N. Y., of pneumonia. Particulars of his last hours have not yet reached us, but we are sure that he died as he lived— a noble, generous, commanding, patriotic man, and an earnest, tender, faithful, childlike Christian.

Beloved friend and Bishop, farewell! Thou hast gone to the land where no misunderstanding exists; where no envious detraction poisons the air with its breath; where all the inhabitants "see as they are seen, and know as they are known"; and where the Lamb appears "in the midst of the throne." Thou hast joined thy fellow-workers who labored to lay true foundations for religion here. Owen, Bannister, Thomas, Blain, Tansy, Maclay, and Guard

have welcomed thee, with hundreds more
of thy companions and friends. If it please
God we shall join thee and them ere long.
Till then, farewell!

JAS. W. WHITING.
Present Superintendent Sunday School.

HISTORY OF SUNDAY SCHOOL.

As we approach the history of the Sunday School we are met by a remarkable fact, which seems to give a historic unity to the school for the thirty-two years of its existence. Four only, of the original or organizing members of the Church, remain—viz: Seneca Jones and wife and J. W. Whiting and wife. The first named was really the first Superintendent, so far as the parentage of the movement is concerned; and the last named is the present Superintendent. Brother Jones and wife resided near the corner of Essex and Folsom streets, where the Folsom Street Church was afterwards erected. Here at their own home, on or about April 14, 1851, they gathered some of the children of the neighborhood, and regularly met them in Sunday School, until the organization of the Society on Market street.

At this time, naturally, the little *Home Mission* was merged into the new movement, and on the first Sunday in January, 1852,

M. C. Briggs, for a brief period in charge of the Society, organized the Sunday School formally, by appointing M. E. Willing its Superintendent.

At the first quarterly meeting of the charge, the pastor, G. S. Phillips, reported the average attendance of scholars as about fifteen, with one hundred volumes in the library. The meetings of the Society and Sunday School were held in what was known as the Happy Valley School House, which was kindly placed at the service of the infant church organization, and continued to shelter the little fledgeling until it found more spacious accomodations in the Bush street School-house the following year. This last named building stood on the site now occupied by H. S. Crocker & Co's stationery store.

The first statistical report furnished, bearing date August 1, 1852, is as follows: Number of scholars, 25; Officers and teachers, 10; Members of Bible class, 5; Total, 40; Volumes in Library, 100; Papers taken, 25. General remarks: "Prospects seem to be brightening."

About this time M. E. Willing resigned the superintendency of the school, and Horace Hoag was chosen to the position.

In December of this year, Mrs. John Burns, now an honored and useful member of our church in San Jose, gathered about fifteen of the younger members of the school into an infant class. She says: "Most of the children of San Francisco were living just about the school-house, in that part of the straggling city known as Happy Valley. The first hymn I taught them was: 'There is a Happy Land, far, far away.' At the close of the school, a bright little boy of five years came to me, and with an anxious countenance said: 'Teacher, is it as *far* to Heaven as it is to the *States*?' He had come all the way from Boston via Cape Horn, and doubtless was feeling unwilling to start on another journey involving so many weeks of weary travel and sea-sickness. The child's name was Hindley. He lived to be a man of thirty years, and then passed to the 'Happy Land' not so very 'far away' as childhood had inferred from the terms of the deathless poem he had sung. I have not regretted the effort made to meet that little class, although it involved the difficult task of treading through the sand, which was so generously stored in drifts and piles all about that part of the young, and yet enterprising city. How often I had to stop and hold my position against the contesting winds and drifting sand, and wait for a 'lull' to enable me to proceed. 'But God was the strength of my heart,' and I was glad to labor for Him, and 'sow in the morn' the seed, which, I trust, will reveal some fruitage in the Heavenly garner."

The above reminds me of the outflow of the heart of a dear personal friend, Rev. Dwight Williams, of the Central New York Conference, which I will venture to insert as a fitting climax to this fragment of the early history of our infant class.

POEM.

The love of a child,
The love of a child,
I know I am oft by the passion beguiled ;
I know it is bliss
To feel its soft kiss,
No balm of affection is sweeter than this ;
And Jesus to win it spread out his dear hands,
And children now love him in heavenly lands.

The child of the poor,
A smile at thy door
May fill his sad heart with joy brimming o'er ;
Oh, do not refrain
From soothing its pain,
Nor send it on morning or pining again ;
Look down in those eyes, and see if there be
No image of gladness to shine back on thee.

Did you know 'twere a bliss,
  Too precious to miss,
When you pass to the realms of the angels from this,
  From little hands white,
  And eyes beaming bright,
To drink the sweet nectar of heaven's delight?
Forever, forever a joy it will be,
A fountain from childhood land flowing to thee.

  Away and away,
  No longer delay;
Find gems that will glisten in heaven's bright day.
  Oh, yes, they will cling,
  To the crowns which you bring,
And cast at the feet of Jesus, your King;
The heart of a child, oh win it by love,
To bask in the sunshine forever above.

  The heart of a child,
  Though wanton and wild,
Oh do not turn from it and leave it defiled,
  But touch if you can,
  By some little plan,
The heart that will beat with the throb of a man,
Oh, win it to love thee where golden years roll,
And love is forever the joy of the soul.

The first infant baptism enrolled in connection with the charge was administered by Bishop Ames, on the 24th of January of this year, while the service was yet held at the Happy Valley School-house, where the Bishop preached his first sermon on the Pacific coast. On this Sabbath the Quarterly Conference was held, and the Sunday school report rendered in connection therewith by G. S. Phillips, Pastor, indicated the following facts: One Sunday school with eighty scholars; fifteen teachers, and one hundred and fifty volumes in the library. This quarterly meeting organized the first Board of Trustees, and the society took organic form as the Second Methodist Episcopal Church of San Francisco.

The growth of the Sunday school is indicated by the fact that the report rendered, bearing date July 30th of the same year, gave the number of scholars 200, with 22 officers and teachers, and 300 volumes in the library. This quarterly meeting recorded the reported purchase of a lot on Market street for church building purposes. The Sunday school had at some time in this year accompanied the church services under whose fostering care it existed to the Bush Street School-house, as before stated.

The fact that in October of this year there is a recorded notice received from the authorities to discontinue the services at this place doubtless had much to do with the purchase above mentioned, and hurried the young and struggling church on its way into the possession and occupancy of a house of its own. We need not follow the property records, which indicate various changes, in tracing the history of this child of the church; suffice it to say the child lived with its parents and was always nestled close to the heart of its "Alma Mater." The reported attendance was very much less immediately after the removal to the new Folsom Street Church, which was dedicated in January, 1854.

William H. Codington here became the superintendent of the school, and began the valuable services he has continued to give Sunday school work in San Francisco Methodism, with the exception of brief absence from the city, until the present time.

The whole of the Bush St. School, however, did not immediately become absorbed into the Folsom street organization, and two schools with respectively 78 and 75 scholars were reported as existing at the time of the first quarterly meeting of the new Folsom street family. This, however, did not long continue; and in June of that year the two branches came together and commenced a more complete and vigorous life in their new home. During a period of peculiar discouragement, financially, the church in debt and paying three per cent. per month interest on five thousand dollars, the Sunday school was the bond that held the church family together, and the inspiration which

carried it over the severest trials. This is
not the only family which has been bound by
the love and obligations which centered in
the child or children of the home, and thus
kept from disintegration and ruin. The
love of a child has saved many a home on
earth, and as the poem inserted has it, may
be "a joy forever."

The Sunday school prospered and grew
in numbers, and was a blessing to the community.

In 1857 Superintendent Codington, still
at the head of the school, reported 18 officers and teachers, and one hundred scholars,
with six hundred volumes in the library,
which certainly was a generous provision of
reading for the school. In addition to this,
however, one hundred and twenty Sunday
School Advocates were taken. In 1858 and
'59 the school continued to prosper and do
its work efficiently, and reported an average
attendance of two hundred scholars, and
twenty-three officers and teachers; the
library still advancing and now having
reached seven hundred volumes. Conversions were also reported in gratifying numbers, and the labors of the faithful officers
and teachers were thus owned of Heaven,
and the real end of Sunday school labor
reached.

In 1860, the record introduces S. S. Sprague as Superintendent, with a Sunday school constitution, and several additional marks of advancement. June 24th of this year the minutes of the teachers' meeting furnish a copy of resolutions duly passed to ascertain the wishes of the children relative to holding a picnic. It is not difficult to predict the result of such a canvass at any time, and the usual result was here reached; and the first picnic, so far as is known, ever enjoyed by the children of our school was held July 4th, 1860, at the Willows, a place of resort located almost exactly where our Grace M. E. Church now stands.

In 1861 W. H. Codington was again chosen Superintendent, and continued to fill the place until 1865. The average attendance for the year of scholars, teachers and officers was 301, with 926 books in the library, and 200 Sunday School Advocates taken. The highest average attendance reached by the school while it remained at Folsom street was in 1862, its last year there, when the figures reached were officers and teachers 32, and scholars 350. In November of this year the property on Folsom street was sold, and the unhoused family found itself, by invitation, under the roof-tree of the Howard Presbyterian Church, at the corner of Jane and Natoma streets. This hospitality was enjoyed until the first Sabbath in January, 1863, when the new basement rooms of the Howard Street Church, where we still abide, opened their doors to receive those for whom they were prepared, and church and Sunday school began to worship and work under their " own vine and fig tree." The growth, incident upon this change was very apparent and striking, and the average attendance reached 480 scholars, with a Bible class of 33 members, and 33 officers and teachers. The church being unfinished, the services were all held in the Sunday school rooms of the church. The annual report of Wm. H. Codington, Superintendent, dated January 4th, 1864, indicates an exceedingly prosperous condition. The secretary reported a roll of 650 officers, teachers and scholars. The minutes contain this allusion to the sad and sudden removal of one of the most esteemed and useful members of the church and Sunday school, viz. : " During the year one of our number has been called to the rest that awaits those who love our Lord. D. S. Howard, our excellent secretary, died October 20th, 1863, and has left a name that will long be remembered among us." We find also this allusion to the connection of the pastor with the work of the school. "The adult Bible class, under the care of our pastor Rev. J. D. Blain, has been fully attended, and proves an excellent source from which to procure teachers as they have been needed in the growth of the school." The teachers, by their punctual attendance and faithful labors, are showing that they have the spiritual welfare of the children at heart, and are deserving the prayers of the church for success in their efforts.

On the 3rd of January, 1865, Charles Goodall was chosen to the position of Superintendent. Dr., afterward Bishop, Jesse T. Peck was pastor of the church and school. The roll numbered 690 in attendance. This was a remarkable showing, when we remember that during the year, viz., in September, 1864, the popular pastor, Rev. J. D. Blain, had been appointed to the new church movement, or mission, which is now the Central M. E. Church on Mission street. The average attendance was diminished by this fact, but the efficiency of the superintendent and his corps of teachers soon carried the school forward again to its former strength. The interruption to the work of the charge, however, by the removal of Dr. Peck, the pastor, in the middle of the Conference year, to New York, worked against the Sunday school as well as the other interests of the church, and the average attendance went down to less than 400 in 1866; which, however, in 1867 went up again to 442 as an average attendance for the year. The records about this time allude to a Mission Sunday school somewhere on Montgomery street, which it was claimed "seceded" from the control of the church, and unfurled the Union Sunday school colors. The spirit of Christian tolerance which prevailed in the school management is indicated by this minute in the records of the school. "If under any name the Word of God is taught to those who in that part of the city so much need it, our donations of 290 volumes of our library books, and the surplus copies of the Sunday School Advocate and Good News, as well as money subscribed, will not have been in vain." January 8th, 1868, W. H. Codington was again elected superintendent, and Dr. H. Cox appears on the records as pastor. This year indicated a slight falling off in attendance, perhaps due to the presence in the church of a Chinese Sunday school, with J. J. Applegate superintendent. If from this cause, the price paid was very insignificant for the privilege of opening the way for the benighted heathen to find the world's and hence *their* Redeemer. The usual prosperity of the school was fully maintained under the faithful and efficient management of John F. Byxbee as Superintendent; during the years 1869–70, with an average attendance of about 430 scholars, with 60 officers and teachers, with 1270 books in the library. Rev. L. Walker was the pastor. There is upon the records this minute. "In memoriam: Bro. E. L. Barber died in January, 1870, and in his removal the Sunday school loses one of its most faithful and efficient teachers." W. H. Codington had charge of the Chinese school, and reported satisfactory results from the labors bestowed in that department of the work.

Chas. Goodall again came to the head of the school in 1871, and continued as superintendent until 1873. The pastor, F. F. Jewell, reported Nov. 11th, 1872, an average considerably smaller than the last figures given in this sketch. The decrease was largely owing to the fact that the charge was without a regular pastor for a large part of the Conference year 1871–2, although the hour upon which it convened was an exceedingly unpopular one at that time. An increased attendance followed a change of hour almost immediately. A system of bi-monthly meetings held in the audience room of the church was in operation, which worked favorably also in bringing the Sunday school and public congregation together, and centering healthy attention upon this part of church work. The average attendance, as given by the pastor's report in Feb., 1873, was 410. At this time the quarterly Conference, impelled by a healthy impulse, created a committee to establish a Mission Sunday school in Hayes Valley, where a school had for a time existed, but had been discontinued for lack of support. That committee reported May 23, 1873, as follows: "Your committee, to whom you entrusted the work of looking out a proper location for a Mission School, after having determined upon starting a school in Hayes Valley, found it impracticable to do so at present, because of a feeling which obtained with some that it would interfere with schools already organized." Thus the work which was but just opening in that locality was postponed for years, and we have nothing now where, ere this, we would have had

HISTORY OF SUNDAY SCHOOL. 183

a strong church organization by the blessing of God.

This year was started a second session of the school, which convened Sabbath A. M. at ten o'clock for instruction in the catechism and song services, and with the expectation that many of the children would remain at the preaching service and assist in the singing. The result was excellent so far as the instruction and other advantages to the children were sought, but the second session was unable to rally teachers for its work, and was given up. The clamorings of the infant class about this time, which, under the care of Mrs. Emily Foster, assisted by Miss Octavia Jewell, had reached a membership of one hundred and fifty, was beginning to be heard for increased accommodations. The pastor in his report to the fourth quarterly Conference of the first year of his pastorate, echoed these cries in these words: "I am compelled to say that the place where the infant class meets is entirely unfit for the purpose, being dark, illy ventilated, and uncomfortably seated. Nothing but the most inexorable necessity should content you to allow such a state of things to continue. Much more than the present capacity is needed for Sunday school, Bible classes, and infant class."

S. Mosgrove, the new Superintendent brought into the school his characteristic energy and enterprise, and the school continued to increase in numbers until the remodeling and enlarging of our Sunday school rooms was a necessity not to be longer ignored; and in connection with other much needed improvements the work was done. The pastor, in the report to the first quarterly Conference of the second year, 1873-74, so changed the tone of his reference to the school accommodations as to say: "The new rooms, or rather the old rooms remodeled, enlarged and refurnished, are among the finest I have ever seen. The increase of light and of comfort in sitting cannot fail of appreciation, and we are expecting to hear our presiding elder, J. W. Ross, say that as our room was the poorest for the purpose of any of our denomination in the city, it is now the best."

The average attendance increased until at the second quarterly Conference of this year the report indicated fully six hundred in steady attendance. This gentle hint to the quarterly Conference appears in the report, which may not be inappropriate at some other time in the history of the school. "If some of the younger teachers were superseded by members of this quarterly Conference and other older members of the church, a higher type of piety might be reached and fuller gospel results realized.

At the end of this Conference year the average attendance had reached 630, with nearly or quite 800 on the roll. The school continued to do its work harmoniously and with success during the following years. As the pastor's report was not spread upon the journal, we have not the figures or facts for the years which have elapsed since the dates above given. J. M. Buffington succeeded Bro. Mosgrove as Superintendent, and introduced some new features into the management which worked advantageously. His blackboard drawings of the lesson thoughts were of the best execution, and assisted greatly in getting the lessons clearly before the minds of the scholars. Bro. Buffington's spirit and efficiency made him appreciated and beloved by the whole school; and the work he did shall furnish a fruitage in "harvest home" on high. J. J. Applegate was elected as his successor, and served a short time only, resigning his place which was filled by the election of J. K. Jones. Bro. Jones introduced the Roll Catechism, which is a feature of our school, and added much of interest to this necessary part of our Sunday-school instruction. His untiring labors in the school, his forcible and emphatic advocacy of Methodist doctrines and usages, were productive of increased spirituality in the school, and many were gathered into the church from the Sunday-school ranks, during the remarkable revival under the labors of Bro. Harrison during Bro. Jones' administration.

The present Superintendent, Bro. J. W. Whiting, one of the organizing members of the church, and yet in the vigor and efficiency of full-orbed manhood was elected to the position last January, and is by his efficiency and popularity justifying the call which placed him there. The following is the order of Superintendents from the origin of our work until the present.

  SENECA JONES.
  M. E. WILLING.
  HORACE HOAG.
  W. H. CODINGTON, 3 terms.
  SAM'L. S. SPRAGUE.
  CHARLES GOODALL, 2 terms.
  JOHN F. BYXBEE.
  SAM'L MOSGROVE.
  J. M. BUFFINGTON.
  J. J. APPLEGATE.
  JOS. K. JONES.
  J. W. WHITING.

HOWARD ST. M. E. SUNDAY SCHOOL.

LIST OF OFFICERS AND TEACHERS, NOV., 1883.

OFFICERS:

PASTOR	REV. F. F. JEWELL
SUPERINTENDENT	J. W. WHITING
SECRETARY	J. KIRK FIRTH
ASSISTANT SECRETARY	W. F. PERKINS
TREASURER	J. B. FIRTH
LIBRARIAN	W. M. INMAN
ASSISTANT LIBRARIAN	W. F. JANTZEN
" "	WILLIAM HARRIS
" "	NAT. T. COULSEN
" "	H. F. PERRY
" "	S. B. MARVIN
LEADER OF SINGING	MISS MAMIE CADY
PIANIST	MISS CARRIE KANOUSE

CLASS NO. 1. Adult Bible class, J. K. Jones, Teacher
" " 2............J. B. Firth, "
" " 3............Mr. Draper, "
" " 4...Misses Miller and Bowman, "
" " 5............J. W. Whiting, "
" " 6........Miss Carrie Jantzen, "
" " 7............Miss A. Wilson, "

LIST OF TEACHERS.

Class No. 8............D. E. McConaughy, Teacher.
" " 9................Miss Lizzie Curry, "
" " 11...............Miss Laura Jones, "
" " 12...............Miss Shearer, "
" " 13...............Mrs. Perkins, "
" " 14...............Miss Maggie Curry, "
" " 15...............Miss S. Jones, "
" " 16...............Mrs. W. B. Cluff, "
" " 19...............Miss Dillie Little, "
" " 22...............Mrs. J. K. Firth, "
" " 25...............Mr. T. B. Smith, "
" " 26...............Miss Nellie Williams, "
" " 29...............R. Pengelly, "
" " 30...............Mrs. J. K. Jones, "
" " 31...............Mr. J. C. Smith, "
" " 32...............Mrs. Burley, "
" " 33...............Miss Annie Thompson, "
" " 34...............Miss Emma Beach, "
" " 37...............Mrs. J. B. Firth, "

SUBSTITUTE TEACHERS:

Mr. Henry Thomas,   Mr. W. M. Whittaker,
Mr. J. H. Stitt (now Teacher Class No. 8).

INFANT CLASS.

Miss Birdie Harris.........................Teacher

ASSISTANT TEACHERS:

Miss Katie Rowe,   Miss Hattie Rowe,
Miss Alice Reynolds,   Miss Alice Stracham.
Leader of infant class singing, Mr. S. M. Batchelder.
150 scholars enrolled in the Infant Class.

REV. F. F. JEWELL, D. D.
Present Pastor.

FRIENDLY HINTS.

My Dear People:—I rejoice to greet you in the name of the Lord, and unite with you in thanksgiving to our Heavenly Father for his many mercies to us as a church and people. Grateful for the past, let us prayerfully look toward our future.

Our mission is to save the world, instrumentally, by bringing the unsaved as soon as possible to the "only wise God, our Savior." No archangel is clothed with a higher or more honorable commission, and we are not to suspend our efforts until the work is done.

Our qualifications for this work must ever consist in personal piety, and that vital alliance with Christ which follows an intelligent, earnest, and entire consecration to Him who gave himself for us.

Let us earnestly seek to understand and experimentally to comprehend the *Genius of Methodism*. One has said Methodism was born in the heart of John Wesley, when, May 24th, 1738, he went to a society meeting in Aldersgate Street, London; and, as he listened earnestly to the reading of Luther's preface to the Romans, in which the great Reformer simply unfolds the doctrine of justification by faith, he suddenly felt his heart strangely warmed—felt that his burden of sin was gone, and that he was a new creature in Christ Jesus—felt "cheered, elevated, excited; transported with sweet affections toward God." From that day the characteristics of Methodism have been:

(1.) *Spirituality.*—Methodism is eminently experimental: its kingdom is the heart. It is nothing if it is not heartfelt, fervent, warm. While it has its distinctive theology, whose salient feature is free-will; and while it has an ecclesiastical polity of its own, whose distinctive feature is the itinerancy; the essential element yet of Methodism always and everywhere is fervent religion. Denominational, without being sectarian or straight-laced, it affiliates cordially and promptly with all heart-felt loyalty to Christ; while holding aloft the shining doctrine of the witness of the Spirit, it encourages that fond assurance of hope that enables one to say: "I know whom I have believed."

I would urge you to a careful, prayerful examination of yourselves. Your personal relations to Christ are of vital importance. It is your privilege to know beyond a doubt that your names are written in the "Book of Life."

To know that your sins are forgiven; that Jesus is your Advocate and Savior; that the Holy Ghost is your Comforter and Sanctifier; that your title to a glorious heavenly inheritance is perfect; is an experience which, dear friend, we urge you to maintain in all its warmth and brightness and power.

If you cannot witness to a present divine assurance that you belong by gracious adoption to the family of God, immediately seek for that witness of the Holy Ghost, whose token is the cry in your heart of "Abba, Father."

That ye may never lack this witness of the Spirit, in the name of the Lord Jesus we exhort you to "go on to perfection." It is your glorious privilege to be saved to to the uttermost; to have Christ so dwell in your hearts that ye, "being rooted and grounded in Him, may be able to comprehend with all saints what is the breadth, and length, and depth, and height, and to know the love of Christ which passeth knowledge, that ye might be filled with all the fullness of God."

Deep Christian experience has been the chief element of power in our church in the past, and is the surety of our success to-day. That Scripture which all the world reads is the epistle which is written on fleshly tables of the heart: epistles which walk and breathe and shine and blaze to the glory of God. Such epistles, known and read of all men, do we exhort you, dear brethren, to become. When your whole life shall be radiant with the Spirit of Christ, then will the darkness in the souls of men about you flee before the power of the light that is in you. Then give most earnest heed to personal spiritual life. This is the interest that overtops all others in life.

A constant walk with God, a constant consciousness of union with Christ, is secured only by a constant, faithful attention to private religious devotion. Then give yourselves much to secret prayer, and to the devout reading of God's word. These are the soul's proper food, and unless you gather this heavenly manna daily, spiritual decay and death will follow your neglect.

ENTIRE SANCTIFICATION.

Methodism differs from other theological systems chiefly in teachings concerning entire sanctification or holiness of heart. This doctrine sustains such a relation to its inception, polity and subsequent history, that any view that does not make this primal must necessarily be a very imperfect one. The calling of Methodism was forecast in the training and spiritual struggles and experience of its founders.

In reading God's word, they were awakened to see that they could not be saved without holiness of heart. Dr. McClintock said in his centenary address: "Knowing exactly what I am saying, I repeat we are the only church in history, from the apostles' time until now, that has put forth as its elemental thought the great central-pervading idea of the whole Book of God, from beginning to end; the holiness of the human soul, heart, mind and will. It may be called fanaticism, but this is our mission."

Methodism began her work declaring her mission to be to "spread scriptural holiness over these lands," and she has achieved her most glorious victories when this doctrine had a place in her pulpit and in the hearts of the people. If, of God as we have fondly believed, then Wesley must have been right about the mission, if there is any relation between a mission and the work it accomplishes; for this was the work of Methodism, spreading scriptural holiness everywhere it went.

She began her work by seeking "the power of godliness." She claimed divine sonship through the blood of the cross, and the witness of the Holy Spirit, and she has had something to say to the world on these subjects. This one fact is so blended with the entire fabric of Methodism, that it cannot be displaced without the subversion of the whole. Her testimony to the reality of entire sanctification, as an experience received by faith subsequent to conversion, is as clear and positive as any testimony ever recorded in her annals. The Wesleys, Fletchers, Bramwells, Carvossos and Cookmans, together with an innumerable throng whose names are as ointment poured forth, are among her best witnesses on the subject of the "power of godliness" in the human soul. "Their feet rested lightly on earth, they trampled on its wealth and pride. They swept through it like apocalyptic angels. They vanished from it like a translation. They have joined the shining ranks of the redeemed that walk with the Lamb in white, over on the immortal shores. The glory of their transfigured lives will shine as the stars forever and ever."

(2.) *Sociality.*—*The social life of the church* is next to its spiritual life, in its relation to its success as a soul-winning agency in the world. It may be misplaced, and relied upon for results without reasonable warrant; or it may be separated from its true relations, and thus involve danger to the church. When you were received into the church, you heard the pastor say: " The fellowship of the church is the communion its members have one with another. Its more particualar duties are to promote peace and unity, to bear one another's burdens, to prevent each other's stumbling, to seek the intimacy of friendly society among themselves, to continue steadfast in the faith and worship of the Gospel, and to pray and sympathize with each other."

It requires no severe analysis to discover much more here than a personal attention to the ordinances of worship, and a coming together in the direct services of religion. The " ends " of this fellowship are elsewhere stated, while here we have what the church supposes—and teaches—to be the duty devolving upon each of its members. The "communion" is its friendly, brotherly intercourse at the table of the Lord, in the social religious meeting, in the walks of business life, in the social gatherings of the brotherhood, and in the closer intimacies of the family and more private circles. And surely, " to seek the intimacy of friendly society among themselves" is sufficiently specific and distinct to require no help for its interpretation. It points directly to social life. There is no need of any radicalism in this matter, or of any exclusion of those who are not united with us in the same church, but simply to be true to the genius and traditions of Methodism. Let an echo of the Ecumenical Conference endorse what I now say:

"I believe that one of the greatest elements of strength in the early Methodists was the fact that wherever you went into a Methodist church, you found yourself not in a sepulcher but in a home. A great deal can be done in the way of heartily welcoming visitors. In the early Methodist chapels no young man went and stood for several minutes at the door, wondering whether there was any seat which he could enter: there were scores of hands ready to be held out to meet him. And, at the close of the service, those to the right and those to the left were prepared to stand by his side, and help him to live a godly, righteous and sober life. This is one way in which the laymen can help us. The preacher cannot, because he is in the pulpit. We should not leave showing strangers into a seat to chapel-keepers; but every layman should be a chapel-keeper. Let no one even approach the door of a Methodist chapel without receiving a hearty welcome there."

"I attend your church now, because when I came there first your folks gave me a welcome. I concluded that they were social people." Such was the reason given by a gentleman to a member of one of our churches for identifying himself with the congregation. He had gone to several places of worship in search of a Sabbath home, without finding one adapted to his wants. He received no recognition either before or after the services, and retired feeling that he was a stranger if not an intruder. But the courtesy shown him by one of the ushers, and the interest manifested in his presence by the cordial salutations he received from several who politely addressed him as he was leaving the place, impressed him with a sense of their kindness, made him to feel that his presence was valued, and gave him assurance that he would find such friends as he would feel at home with. It is not by simply suspending the word "Welcome" in the vestibules of our churches that this result is to be accomplished. There should be a polite, personal recognition of the stranger, and such a greeting as will not fail to convey the impression that sincere pleasure is felt in the presence of the new-comer. By taking pains to make the acquaintance of a stranger, and by giving him an introduction to one or two members of the church, ties will quickly be formed that will hold to a congregation not a few who are now strolling from place to place under a miserable feeling of isolation, and which will prove to be one of the strongest links in the chain of means and influences ordained to draw them to God and bind them to his service.

"When the First Presbyterian Church of New York stood in Wall street, Robert Lennox, then an eminent merchant, was a member. He took a great interest in young men, especially those who were strangers.

He invariably on Sundays took the position of usher, welcomed all new-comers, and escorted them to comfortable seats. Standing in the vestibule one day he saw a young man coming up the steps, evidently a stranger, and with the air of one who felt himself an intruder.

"The frank and hearty merchant met the young man on the threshold, gave him his hand, and told him he was glad to see him that morning in the house of the Lord.

"'You are a stranger, I presume,' he said.

"'Yes; this is my first Sabbath in New York, and my mother charged me to reverence the house of the Lord.'

"Just in from his country home the young man was not over-dressed. Mr. Lennox escorted him up the centre aisle and seated him in his own pew.

"The next morning the young man went to a business house, to see if he could get a small bill of goods. He gave his references.

"Did I not see you in Mr. Lennox's pew yesterday?' said the merchant.

"'I don't know, sir. A gentleman gave me a seat in church, and sat down beside me.'

"'Well, young man, that gentleman was Robert Lennox, and I will trust any young man whom Mr. Lennox seats in his pew.'

"That young man became an eminent merchant. To the day of his death he said: 'I owe all I am in this world to that Sunday when Mr. Lennox invited me to sit in his pew.'"

This spirit should more than anywhere else characterize the prayer meetings and class meetings of the Church. The true idea of the Church is that it is a family—God's family. Its members are children of one Father, and brothers and sisters one of another. A prayer-meeting, therefore, is a family meeting. It is a reunion of brothers and sisters. The service is of the character of a feast; and we all know that after feasting comes talking and exhibition of good nature. After the formal portion of the service is over, brethren, why not stay and have an informal service of your own? Talk of whatever the Spirit suggests; tell your joys and your sorrows, your hopes and your fears, one to another. "Laugh with those who laugh, and weep with those who weep." At least stay long enough, after the formal service, to shake hands with the pastor and with each other, and greet any stranger that may chance to have dropped in among you of an evening. Lubricate the wheels of your Church machinery with the "oil of gladness," and you will be astonished at the ease with which all its parts will soon be working together. "Salute every saint in Christ Jesus."

(3.) *Family Religion.*—Whilst Romanism and some forms of Protestantism make the church the instructor and guide of the child, Methodism has always emphasized the importance of family religion. I beseech you, dearly beloved, to make your homes the sanctuaries of God. Let nothing destroy your family altars. Cultivate hearthstone religion, that your children may grow up taught in the Word, and familiar with the voice of prayer and praise. Let the aroma of your devotion penetrate all your family relations. Let all who dwell in your homes behold the great satisfaction which you have in the service of God. Especially, by the beauty of a holiness that puts its glory on all your words and acts, by the charm of a piety that is ever full of hope and of good cheer, by the power of a faith at once triumphant and joyful, commend the religion of Jesus to all your household. If we are to acknowledge

God in all our ways, if we are to commit our interests to his keeping in the confidence that He cares for us and will direct our steps, certainly this ought to be done in the family if anywhere. All the excuses that are offered on the part of those who have no recognition of God in the house; who sit down to the table morning, noon, and night—a table spread with the bounties of God's providence, and neither ask God's blessing upon the food, nor thank him for what He does for them, feeding themselves like brute beasts off from the bounties of God's providence; who build no family altar, who never call their children together to join in the reading of God's word, and in prayer for Heaven's blessing—what wonder if God's face is against them? Has he not threatened to pour out his indignation on the heathen, and on the families that call not on his name? There can be no *Christian* home without a family altar, from which daily rises the incense of prayer and praise. Let care be used that the altar-fires never go out. Let each member of the family, so far as may be, share in the exercises of family devotion. Let all the members of the household be present. Let the children grow up under these influences, and when the heads of the household fall by death, the family altar will not fall into ruin.

As an ally in your parental priesthood and ministry we urge you to use the public means of grace. We believe in the Sunday School, and rejoice in the work it is doing. Let it have your confidence—your sympathy—your support—your co-operation—your prayers—and your presence. If there was ever any opposition to Sunday Schools it has given way before the manifestly good work they have been doing in all the years since Wesley said: "Who knows but some of these schools may become nurseries for Christians?"

There is, however, an evil which must be guarded against. In some places the children generally neglect to attend the preaching services. The Sunday-school is all in all to them, and they seem to consider it as "the children's church." They regard the preaching service as intended solely for grown-up people and not at all for them, and they stay away from it. It is not difficult to foresee the result of this neglect. These children will soon be too old—in their own opinions—to attend the school as scholars, and unless they have already formed the habit of attending the preaching service, they will drift away from all church influences.

As yet the evil is confined to certain localities. But it is an evil which is spreading, and ought to be promptly checked. For the Sunday school is certainly not a substitute for the public ministrations of the Word. Teaching in the class is a good thing, but preaching includes teaching and something more. The orator is more than an instructor. Both parents and teachers should use their influence, and even their authority, if they have any, to bring the children to the public service in the house of God. If the child cannot attend both the preaching service and the Sunday school, then the preference should be given to the former. On this point our convictions are deep and clear.

Certain it is that the founders and first promoters of Sunday schools never dreamed of drawing away the children from the regular public services of the church.

And now we say, as Dr. Vincent and other eminent and enthusiastic Sunday school authorities have said and repeated: "If children cannot attend both Sunday school and public worship, it is in every way better for them to attend the latter. It is now the hour in their lives when their most powerful, determining, and persistent impressions are received. The habit of associating the Sabbath with ideas of special sanctity, of regular attendance upon the sanctuary, of the importance of public worship, is now to be formed.

"If this habit is not formed, we shall see what we do now see in the instance of numbers of Christian families—a most extraordinary looseness of sentiment and habit in reference to the Sabbath and the instruction of the pulpit."

As akin to family religion and its maintenance in the home and in the hearts of the young, let me call attention to the subject of

POPULAR AMUSEMENTS.

The secular press is employed in publishing and puffing them without discrimination as to moral character and tendencies. Some other churches as well as our own are concerned about them, because of their bearing on the religious life of their younger members. The initiatory precept of Christianity is self-denial; and the General Rule of our Discipline forbids the "taking of such diversions as cannot be used in the name of the Lord Jesus." But the growing laxity among Christian professors in regard to worldly amusements, and the plausible but fallacious apologies by which they seek to defend them, led our General Conference to define more specifically what is meant by "Sinful Amusements!" And hence, we find in the new Discipline, under the head of "Un-Christian and Imprudent Conduct," the following specific items, viz: Dancing, playing at games of chance, attending theaters, horse races, circuses, dancing parties, or patronizing dancing schools, or taking such other amusements as are of questionable moral tendency. It is a painful reflection that it should have been deemed a necessity to incorporate this detailed enumeration in our Discipline.

What renders the subject one of deep concern to all true Christians, and to parents who value the proper training of their children, is, that these amusements come to us in many instances under auspices and with such sanctions as to give to them the character of respectability, or they come in the name of charity, or as appreciative returns for public benefits. Billiards, cards, dances, charades and tableaux scenes are counted respectable, because they are introduced into private families which are reckoned as respectable. Balls are gotten up in the interest of some asylum, or some charitable institution; some fireman's or military company; and these make their appeals to the better fellings of our nature, because of service rendered or to be rendered. Worst of all is the fact, that some churches and members of Protestant churches take such low views of the nature of Christianity as to imagine that these things are at all consistent with the Christian name.

With God's word in one hand and the Methodist Discipline in the other, let us resolve that by our example, as well as our teaching, we will endeavor to develop a correct and healthful sentiment among our people on this subject, so that in respect to amusements, as well as in regard to morals and religion, the church may stand forth as the light and leader of the world.

And let none forget their covenant obligations taken at baptism, " to renounce the devil and all his works: the vain pomp and glory of the world, with all covetous desires of the same, and the carnal desires of the flesh, so as not to follow or be led by them"; and your agreement on becoming a member of the church—to keep all our rules of holy living.

In considering the home life and its influence upon the character and destiny of its constituency, let us call your attention to one of the potential agencies of this age in formation of character—the

LITERATURE OF THE HOME.

In doing so, we would earnestly urge upon your attention the value and claims of the religious publications of our church. An active, aggressive church must have an intelligent membership. We are sure you can not fill the measure of your usefulness as Christians, unless you read not only the publications of the secular press, but the periodicals of our church as well. And further, the only safeguard for your household from the dissipating, demoralizing influence of vicious reading, is in the abundance of pleasing, profitable and Christian literature which our church so abundantly provides for you.

In your general reading, do not accept what first comes to hand, but carefully select that which will most tend to your soul's health and comfort. See that your Sunday school and families are properly supplied with the literature of our own church. Other churches furnish much valuable reading, but our own home-born Methodist writers have a peculiar aptness for stating and teaching the doctrines of free grace. Take special pains to induce your children to read only good books, and to reject as poisonous and destructive the low and corrupt literature of the day. Purchase and read our approved Methodist standard works, that thereby you may become rooted and grounded in the faith of the Gospel.

I can find no better presentation of the importance of this admonition than is couched in the language of the pastoral address from the Bishops to our last General Conference:

"Parental supervision of the literature of childhood and youth is of equal importance with jealous watchfulness over the companions allowed to them. We fear that thousands of parents know very little of the reading of their children, and they allow unchallenged, loose, and even licentious literature the freedom of their homes, which poisons the thoughts, perverts the imagination and depraves the hearts and lives of the children of the church. We should know what they read by providing freely the choicest publications at our command. Money expended thus is money saved, with purity retained and integrity added. Our own publishing houses will amply supply this demand. The duty assigned to our pastors, superintendents, and Sabbath school committees, to decide what books shall be used in our schools, if faithfully performed, would protect our libraries; and we fear that a neglect of this supervision has admitted improper reading thereto in some instances."

CONCLUSION.

And now, let me conclude this already too lengthy address as I began it, by assuring you that to meet your obligations you need the joyful and abiding witness of the Spirit that you are wholly the Lord's, and that your will is in complete harmony with the will of God, and that the blood of Jesus Christ cleanses you from all unrighteousness. And we gladly assure you that it is the duty and privilege of every child of God to lay hold, by faith, of the exceeding great and precious promises of God's word, so as to become "complete in Christ," and "be filled with all the fullness of God." For this is the end of our ministry among you, "the perfecting of the saints," "the perfect man," "the measure of the stature of the fullness of Christ," "whom we preach, warning every man and teaching every man in all wisdom that we may present every man perfect in Christ Jesus." "And this we pray, that your love may abound more and more in knowledge and in all judgment, that ye may approve things that are excelent, that ye may be sincere and without offense till the day of Christ, being filled with the fruits of righteousness, which are of Jesus Christ, unto the glory and praise of God." "For what is our hope or joy or *crown* of rejoicing? Are not even ye in the presence of our Lord Jesus Christ at his coming? For ye are our *glory* and *joy*." And now, brethren, we commend you to God and the word of his grace which is able to build you up, and to give you an inheritance among all them that are sanctified.

Affectionately your pastor,

F. F. JEWELL.

ADDITIONAL MEMBERS.

The following names have been added to the record of present members, since the form containing the record was printed, viz:

Maggie Nelson.
W. S. Clark, M. D.
E. L. Paulding, M. D.
Emma F. Bugby.
C. Will Beers.
Arzelia Beers.
Mary B. Quigg.
Henry Stinger.
Timenia Conant.
Cornelia Perry.

www.ingramcontent.com/pod-product-compliance
Lightning Source LLC
Chambersburg PA
CBHW021826230426
43669CB00008B/883